Spelling: Caught or Taught?

by Margaret L. Peters
Tutor, Cambridge Institute of Education

LONDON AND HENLEY
ROUTLEDGE AND KEGAN PAUL
ATLANTIC HIGHLANDS, N.J.: HUMANITIES PRESS

First published 1967
by Routledge and Kegan Paul Ltd
39 Store Street
London WC1E 7DD and
Broadway House, Newtown Road
Henley-on-Thames
Oxon, RG9 1EN
Reprinted 1976

Printed in Great Britain by
Unwin Brothers Limited, Old Woking, Surrey

© Margaret L. Peters 1967

No part of this book may be reproduced
in any form without permission from
the publisher, except for the quotation
of brief passages in criticism

ISBN 0 7100 4218 3 (c)
ISBN 0 7100 4211 6 (p)

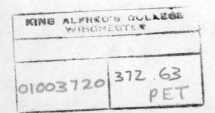
KING ALFRED'S COLLEGE
WINCHESTER

01003720 372.63
PET

Spelling: Caught or Taught?

KING ALFRED'S COLLEGE
WINCHESTER
ENGLISH DEPARTMENT

KA 0100372 0

THE STUDENTS LIBRARY OF EDUCATION

GENERAL EDITOR:
Lionel Elvin
formerly Director,
University of London Institute of Education

EDITORIAL BOARD:
Psychology of Education:
Professor Ben Morris
University of Bristol

Philosophy of Education:
Professor Richard S. Peters
University of London

History of Education:
Professor Brian Simon
University of Leicester

Sociology of Education:
William Taylor
Director,
University of London Institute of Education

Method and Curriculum Studies:
Professor Paul Hirst
University of Cambridge

Interdisciplinary Studies:
Professor Richard S. Peters
University of London

The founding Series General Editor was the late J. W. Tibble,
Emeritus Professor of Education, University of Leicester.

General editor's introduction

This series has been designed to meet the needs of students of Education at Colleges of Education and at University Institutes and Departments. It will also be valuable for practising teachers and educationists. The series takes full account of the latest developments in teacher-training and of new methods and approaches in education. Separate volumes will provide authoritative and up-to-date accounts of the topics within the major fields of sociology, philosophy and history of education, educational psychology, and method. Care has been taken that specialist topics are treated lucidly and usefully for the non-specialist reader. Altogether, the Students' Library of Education will provide a comprehensive introduction and guide to anyone concerned with the study of education, and with educational theory and practice.

Spelling is an essential skill, if children are to be able to write freely and adventurously without hesitation or circumlocution. Can this skill be caught or must it be taught? If it is to be taught, what are the most economical methods? Research in the last half-century into whether spelling can be learned incidentally, and into the teaching of spelling, has been largely ignored in schools, but the research of the last few years can no longer be neglected. In this book it is reviewed and made intelligible to the practising teacher. Particular attention is paid to recent work on the probability of letters appearing in words in certain sequences, and implications are drawn for the teaching of spelling, which, it is argued, is not a hindrance to, but a pre-requisite of creative writing.

J.W.T.

My thanks are due to the Cambridge Institute of Education for the facilities provided for research, and to the teachers connected with the Institute's Remedial Centre for their co-operation and encouragement.

My thanks are also due to William Latham, of the University of London Institute of Education, for reading and constructively criticizing the manuscript and to Miss Christine Hexter for invaluable clerical assistance.

M.L.P.

Contents

1
The spelling problem

Some primary school teachers were recently asked for their views on the teaching of spelling. Most thought that the teaching of spelling occurred incidentally when children were encouraged to write about their interests, with the enlargement of vocabulary involved in such activities. Phrases such as 'when the need arises', 'association of ideas' appeared. There was conviction that spelling was a means to an end, and that it should only be a servant of creative writing. There was little evidence of actual instruction in spelling. Comments occasionally appeared such as, 'I am in a complete state of uncertainty about the problem of spelling. Please help if you can'. Such a *cri de coeur* points to the dilemma in which teachers have been placed in relation to the teaching of spelling.

The dilemma has arisen because, for many, spelling, like reading and writing, is associated with what has come to be known as formal teaching, in which certain things were taught as part of a tradition. There was no rationale, no thinking about why they were being taught, merely a long-standing tradition, and part of that tradition was the teaching of reading and spelling. The phrase 'formal teaching' usually, if mistakenly, implies certain methods such as stereotyped instruction, drill and rote learning. So teachers brought up in a modern child-centred primary school climate are faced with a dilemma.

On the one hand they see that given the realities of school life at the present, such a streaming, 11 + selection and 'O' levels, a child is severely handicapped if he cannot spell correctly. They also feel deeply, if obscurely, that spelling has some importance although they are not quite sure what, and they comfort themselves with the doctrine that spelling can be picked up incidentally while attending to more important things like creative writing. What such teachers have not examined is whether spelling is picked up in this way, or to what extent. They also have rather an undifferentiated view of learning and do not sufficiently appreciate that different things have to be learnt in different ways. Obviously talk of insight and discovery has application in relation to the learning of things like mathematics and science, and in modern educational theory there has been much more concentration on this kind of learning, but the learning of skills and its importance has been rather neglected. In learning a skill like reading or spelling, practice is of cardinal importance, and talk about insight has very little point when confronted with the anomalies of English spelling, in which words often do not conform to any known principle. The learning of skills, however, is obviously not *just* a matter of practice; for there are other very important factors as well which will be discussed later.

Much of this monograph will be concerned with the factual question of the extent to which a skill such as spelling can be picked up or caught. Before however, embarking on the examination of this sort of question a few preliminary remarks must be made about the case for teaching spelling at all. It may well be the case that there are good reasons for learning to spell which the traditional teacher never bothered to make explicit. It may also be the case that there is something to be said for lessons of a formal type in teaching this as well as other skills, which must supplement other more informal ways of handing them on.

What then are the reasons for learning to spell correctly?

The case for good spelling

It need scarcely be said that there are many bad reasons, educationally speaking, which lead to an insistence on correct spelling. Most of them derive from the tendency on the part of parents to treat spelling ability as a status symbol. In the first place the ability to spell correctly may indicate to parents that a good start has been made on the educational ladder. Secondly the parents themselves, like many other adults, are starkly confronted with the problem of spelling when a letter has to be written or a form filled in. It is natural, therefore, for them to regard spelling as important; for this is a test of their own literacy, education and status. It is, socially speaking, in the same category as a good accent. It is an intangible but essential symbol of status. It is not surprising, therefore, that parents tend to fuss over their child's spelling; for they regard their child to a certain extent as an extension of themselves, and if their child cannot spell, this inadequacy reflects on them.

A third bad reason for paying attention to spelling does not derive so directly from concern for status. It is much more connected with pedantry, with a nonfunctional neurosis about detail. In cases like this an understandable concern for accuracy is extended well beyond the bounds of what is necessary for communication. Odd slips and minor mistakes, that do not impede communication at all, are dwelt upon and fussed over. The delight the child takes in writing a letter, and his spontaneity of expression is spoilt by the parent's constant correction of spelling mistakes.

3

These, then, are some of the bad reasons parents have for insisting on good spelling. Obviously, however, if there were not also some good reasons for spelling correctly, the subject of spelling would not be one to which parents or teachers should give attention, still less would it be a suitable subject for a monograph such as this.

What then are the good reasons? First of all there are reasons connected with communication and consideration for others. If spelling is poor and careless, communication suffers; for either the reader is constantly held up through having to puzzle out what a word is, or else is positively misinformed. The degree of precision necessary in spelling is obviously closely connected with ease and smoothness of communication. There is secondly, the connected question of courtesy. Not to speak clearly, not to write legibly and not to spell correctly are marks of discourtesy. Bad spelling is just as bad in this respect as mumbling over a telephone. Thirdly there is the question of habit-formation. Spelling is a skill in which it is necessary to be precise, and precision generally is one of the main virtues educated people have to acquire. Precision is not only important from the point of view of the other person, the person who is going to receive the communication and read what is written, but also from the point of view of the person who wishes to communicate. The presumption is that some transfer of training occurs, and that what is transferred in a skill such as spelling is not a technique but a habit of care. A casual attitude manifests itself in handwriting, in punctuation, in spelling, and in poorly constructed sentences and paragraphs. Careful attention to any one of these aspects of writing may well affect the others.

Fourthly there is another very important educational reason for good spelling which is connected with freedom to write. 'Creative writing' is now fashionable. Some teachers accept 'creative writing' unmoved by the appearance, the

4

spelling, or the punctuation, provided the content is exciting and vivid. Yet it is only when we have achieved that
machine-like spelling of which Schonell spoke, spelling that
is automatic, predictable, and infallible, that we are really
free to write with confidence, with no backward glances to
see if a word 'looks right', and with no offering of a less
precise synonym or phrase because the right one is difficult
to spell. The competent and hence confident speller will
explore new ways of expressing himself. He will experiment with new words, which up till now may have been
passive. The new words tentatively tried out in conversation are becoming active. For the competent and confident
speller these words will become active on paper, for he,
accustomed to the likelihood of certain sequences of letters
in English, will, from his experience in handling such
sequences, make a confident and fairly accurate attempt.
But the poor speller may avoid using the new and exciting
word. He may use a simpler and less precise circumlocution.

Far from being freed to write creatively by ignoring
spelling and similar conventions, some children, and adults,
are only freed to write when they have learnt to spell
correctly. It is like a pianist who can only interpret the
music when he knows it 'by heart'. Only when he has
reached the stage of muscular recall, and no longer has to
go via the medium of visual recognition, only when he is
unworried by the intricacies of the written score or by the
technicalities of fingering, and the fingers move in sequence,
can he attend not to the symbols but to the sound that
emerges. In the same way the writer, unworried by the
intricacies of spelling, can write as freely as he can speak,
can expand his ideas, can give examples, figures of speech,
confidently and adventurously.

This sort of freedom in writing is a necessary condition
of academic education, one indication among many that a

child can profitably proceed with it. In a streamed school this can have important consequences; for other things being equal, a child who spells correctly and can attend to the content of what he is writing, is more likely to achieve promotion to a higher stream than one whose teacher, often unintentionally, raises her eyebrows at poor spelling before she can attend to the content of the composition. An example of this was an eleven-year-old boy, a very unco-operative and aggressive non-reader who had been referred to the Remedial Centre at the age of nine, with an I.Q. measured by the Terman-Merrill Revision of the Stanford Binet Scale in the region of 109. At $10\frac{1}{2}$ years his reading age had reached $11\cdot2$ years but his spelling age was only $7\cdot9$ years. He was given a year's intensive course in remedial spelling and when he entered the Secondary Modern School he was put in an 'A' stream. This boy achieved an impressive array of 'O' levels including a Grade I in English Language, three 'A' levels with an 'A' and distinction in Physics and is now reading Physics at the University.

As Douglas (1964), has shown, educational advantage and opportunity is strongly influenced by the stream in which a child is placed. It may well be that without efficient spelling this boy would not have qualified for, or maintained his place in the 'A' stream, since he would not have achieved the freedom to write unhampered by spelling problems. Many children, however, never achieve this freedom, and as adults, escape somehow from revealing their ineptitude. They may write simply; they may avoid the words they use in everyday speech, because these are too difficult to spell; they may not write at all.

What is involved in spelling?

Why does a poor speller have to go such lengths? What is

6

preventing him from writing as surely and accurately as the good speller? Consider the case of a ten-year-old writing a 'thank-you letter' for a present; 'Thank you very much for the lovely . . .' All is well up to now. The child has met and used, first passively, then actively, all these words. But now he is faced with the new word. The present he has received is a toy flying saucer. He may avoid writing it by saying 'present' which he can spell. He may offer 'space-ship' which he can attempt. He may try the word itself. Of 967 ten-year-olds attempting the word 'saucer', 462 children wrote it successfully. The remaining 505 offered between them 209 alternative spellings. If they had been presented with the word saucer to *read*, it would have been read correctly, according to recent norms (Andrews, 1964) of Schonell's Graded Word Reading Test by 71% of eight-year-olds, and this in a word-reading test, where the words are divorced from context. Asked to write it, only 47% of ten-year-olds were able to write it correctly. To read a word we look at it and if we do not immediately recognize its pattern as 'saucer', we isolate it into learned phonic elements, s-au-ce-r, which we say, and the meaning *hits us* as we read it in the context of the sentence, provided, that is, that we have heard, or better still used the word before. Reading is from the unknown via the context to the known. Spelling is from the known to the unknown. How can we make this unknown known?

To spell a word we hear it, or image it aurally or with articulatory movements, sub-vocally, and then we are faced with the many and various combinations, particularly of vowels that are possible alternatives, au, aw, or, ow, ser, cer, sa, sir. The alternatives demanded in the complicated competitions devised by detergent and cereal companies are not as puzzling as the alternatives presented in writing an unknown word. They at least offer clues however remote and misleading. Many words to be spelt offer none.

If clues are given in an unknown word that has to be spelt, they are given in the sound, but the same sound can be written in many ways. The known meaningful sound has to be written in an unknown way. In reading, the child or less competent reader is concerned with what a word sounds like. The unknown word is being transformed into the known meaningful sound. Spelling, unlike reading, is encoding a familiar and meaningful sound into a strange and unpredictable code. And as long as we cling to the sound of the message rather than the code, in other words the sounds comprising the word, not the elements of the code, we cannot possibly write the word in code. It would be safe and reliable if the English language were entirely and unexceptionally phonemically regular. The English language is largely but not wholly phonemically regular. From a study of words used by children themselves in the course of their writing, as collected by Edwards and Gibbon (1963), it looks as if as many as 90% of the words they use are phonemically regular—Groff (1961) looking at the New Iowa Spelling Scale (1954), which had been constructed from the written communications of adults and children, puts the percentage at 70%, and Hanna and Moore (1953) analysing the regular phonemes (the smallest unit of representation used in alphabet writing—the irreducible meaningful speech sound) in children's speech and writing found that 80% were represented by regular spelling. So it looks as if between 1 and 3 words in every 10 are phonemically irregular. Simply to transfer our knowledge of sounds to spelling, would be fatal with the 10-30% of phonemically irregular words—so too with the many phonemically regular words that could have quite reasonable alternatives, e.g. stayed could reasonably be written staid or stade; great could well be grate or grait.

The only reason that any of us ever get beyond the precariousness of such coding is that we have learned to look attentively and selectively. As humans sight is our preferred sense; we rely on looking to check almost everything we do. We certainly rely on looking to check the correctness or incorrectness of our spelling. The boy mentioned above, was over the last fence when he said: 'Lemme write it down and see what it looks like!' He had, by this time, learnt the look of the most likely sequences of letters in our language. If, for example, we know that in the word 'courteous', the 'e' is followed by 'ous' not 'us' we are prepared by our knowledge of precedent to write 'ous' in the word 'beauteous'. We implicitly associate structurally similar words. This is because the probability of words conforming to spelling precedent is very high, and it is by becoming familiar with spelling precedents that we become good spellers. In other words familiarity with a coding system is half the battle in learning to spell.

Wallach (1963), investigating the coding system by which children learn to spell, presented good and poor eleven-year-old spellers with briefly exposed flash cards, and asked them to write what they saw. Some flash cards bore random strings of six letters e.g. D N E H P S or G W D N M L. Some were groups of letters that were very similar to English words, such as A P H Y S T or E P I D O L. These can be evolved in party-game manner by one person thinking of a word but only divulging three consecutive letters e.g. T E R. The next person thinks of a word including T E R but adds a letter and drops the first, offering E R V and so on

TER
ERV
RVI
VIC

producing a nonsense word that reflects the probability structure of English very closely. Indeed, apart from the important fact that it is not derived etymologically, such a word could easily have been an English word.

The experiment revealed that for random words there was very little difference between good and poor spellers, but good spellers were found to recognize nonsense words resembling English much more readily than poor spellers. The good spellers had learned a general coding system based on the probabilities of letters occurring in certain sequences in English.

This is the case in any language, though there is no transfer from one language to another, because the spelling conventions of one language are quite different from the spelling conventions of another. Bruner (1953) quotes an experiment he conducted with Harcourt at an International Seminar on the ability to reproduce random strings of letters and nonsense words approximately closely to various languages. There was no difference in ability to handle random strings, but a real difference in ability, favouring one's mother tongue in reproducing nonsense in one's own language. It is easy to place such nonsense words as M J O L K-KOR, K L O O K, G E R L A N C H, O T I V A N C H E, TRI-A N O D E, F A T T A L O N I, etc. As Bruner says, 'When one learns a language one learns a coding system that goes beyond words.' This coding system consists of the most probable combination of letters in words, the groups of letters that tend to go together. The good speller, then, has learnt the probable sequences of letters in words in his own language and these he has learned visually. But the young child, without much experience of the look of words, has a long way to go before he can unhesitatingly select the correct sequence from the various possible alternative letter sequences.

We hear words before we speak them. We speak them before we write them down. The sound of the word precedes the appearance by a very long way, and much visual experience of words is necessary before the individual can select the right one of the many possible alternatives for any unphonetic, or phonetic but irregular, English words, and before the serial probabilities of English words are so fixed that he unfailingly selects the right one. It will be deduced then, that familiarity with serial probability will be derived mainly from reading experience, in other words, that ability to spell may well be 'caught' in the process. The role of incidental learning in spelling has consequently been one of the main pre-occupations of research workers, and this must now be considered.

How is good spelling achieved?

Spelling, we have observed, is unlike reading. Reading is from the unknown via the context to the known. Spelling is from the known to the unknown. How can we make this unknown known? How can we achieve the machine-like movements that are automatic, predictable and infallible? Often parents are confronted by the reassurance, 'He'll learn to spell when he reads more.' Yet there are many well-read and even literary people who still cannot spell. This is the problem behind the role of incidental learning in spelling. Must children be taught to spell? Or can spelling be 'caught' in the process and practice of reading?

As early as 1897, when the teaching of spelling was a universal practice, the possibilities of its being 'caught' were beginning to be considered. Rice, in that year, wrote an article called, 'The futility of the spelling grind', and this was followed up by for example, Cornman (1902) criticizing the systematic teaching of spelling and suggesting, with statistical evidence, that spelling could be approached through other activities such as written work and reading. Though the possibility of spelling being 'caught' rather than 'taught' was challenged soon after by Wallin

(1910) with further statistical evidence in favour of the 'taught' rather than 'caught' school, the controversy had come to stay, simmering in America, but not boiling until the second quarter of the century with Grace Fernald, who in *Remedial Techniques in the Basic School Subjects* (1943, 206) emphasized that 'the most satisfactory spelling vocabulary is that supplied by the child himself' in the course of his own expression. Kyte (1948) supported this view with reservations, advocating the withdrawal of good spellers from formal spelling lessons. Even these, he said, would need to be regularly tested, to ensure that they maintained their competence.

Meanwhile in 1941 in England, Nisbet had mitigated the extremism of Fernald by pointing out that children are likely to 'catch' only one new word out of every twenty-five they read. With older people who are unsophisticated readers, this may also be true, but with serious, slower, more focussed readers such as students, the gain in spelling ability from mere reading could be expected to be greater, particularly in more technical words that may be new to the student, who might pick up the spelling from the significant etymology of the word. Gilbert (1935) found that college students' spelling certainly improved as they read, the extent of the improvement depending on the type of reading and the reader's purpose. Words that had been recently brought to their attention were 'caught' more effectively than words encountered more remotely, and good spellers learned more words than poor spellers.

The role of incidental learning had become respectable. 'Incidental learning is indirect learning,' wrote Hildreth (1956, 33), 'which takes place when the learner's attention is centred not on improving the skill in question, but on some other objective . . .' and qualifies this a moment later with, 'Teachers should not think of incidental learning and integrated teaching as excluding systematic well organized drill. Rather from the child's attempts to write will come evidence of his need for systematic word study.' So not only the spelling will be 'caught', but the need to learn to spell also.

From the evidence so far, then, it looks as if:

(a) Not all children need formal spelling lessons, though the competence of any such children in spelling must be regularly tested. (Kyte, 1948)

(b) Children are likely to learn how to spell (catch) only about 4% of the words they read. (Nisbet, 1941)

(c) 'Catching' words incidentally seems to occur when children's attention is centred on some object other than improving the skill itself. (Hildreth, 1956)

(d) The casual experience of words in reading lessons is, in the case of young and backward children, insufficient for recording permanent impressions. (Schonell, 1942)

(e) College students' spelling improves by reading, particularly of words brought to their attention. Better spellers learn more new words through reading than poor spellers. (Gilbert, 1935)

It looks then, as if spelling is not simply 'caught' by reading.

A second possibility might be that it is partly picked up by listening. But this is obviously a very implausible suggestion. Only in the case of words that have no possible phonic alternatives, is listening of service to correct spelling. With all other words, listening offers no clue. Even in a word such as 'where' (only the Scots and the pedantic sound the h) we are given no auditory clue. So many poor spellers confuse it with 'wear' and even the shorter-vowelled 'were', or confuse 'off' and 'of', in spite of the difference in sound. How much more do words sounding, at any rate to the English, exactly the same (words such

13

as 'there', and 'their', or 'fir' and 'fur') confuse the poor speller. When the poor speller is confronted by a multi-syllabic word, he may well produce an auditory image of the word and separate it into syllables which can be written out one at a time, even though many of these syllables present the possibility of several alternative spellings.

In the days when Spelling Bees were popular, one could identify the victims' methods of attack, in other words whether they were relying on visual or auditory memory. The visualizers read off the word quickly, and usually correctly. Those who relied on auditory memory, spelled syllabically, and the listener was aware of the point of uncertainty . . . 'sacrilegious' would be spelt, 'sacril'— and then uncertainly, 'lig' or 'leg'? Unsupported by other imagery, this is a precarious means to spelling.

It has already been seen that attending to the sound of the word can help in spelling most words, but it is in that small proportion of phonemically irregular words and that bigger proportion of words that, though regular, have some reasonable alternative, that auditory attention is no use. And there is no sense in relying on a system that breaks down just when one needs it most.

If looking alone were enough to make us into good spellers, and if indeed the reader looked at each word, reading would be the answer, and we have shown this only to be the case with older people who had a mental set towards their particular subject or interest, and in the case of those who are good spellers already, for whom just to look was often enough to improve their spelling ability even further. Just looking does not seem to be enough. Spelling ability comes no more from being able to see than being able to hear. Hartmann (1931) showed that spelling ability was not affected by how far or how well one could see, yet there was one special aspect of seeing that was closely related to spelling, one special reaction, that affected spelling. He showed that if meaningful words were exposed on a tachistoscope, or more simply on flash cards of the kind used in schools, more were taken in as wholes by good spellers than by poor spellers. This is possibly because good spellers exercise their imagery. Having perceived a word pattern or configuration, they hold on to this and, while holding on to it, examine it, observing the characteristics of this particular word-form. And training in visual imagery can improve spelling. It has been shown that spelling is improved by as little as two weeks' training in visual imagery, the effects showing a year later when imagery trained groups scored significantly higher on spelling tests than untrained groups (Radaker, 1963). This training in visual imagery is an example of how one can direct the attention of the individual to visual characteristics, to the appearance of the word, and this seems to be a very efficient way of exploiting our preferred sense.

That vision plays a large part in good spelling has been shown in the large number of poor spellers who have reported that they had some defect of vision (Murray, 1919). Spache (1940e) collected reported cases where improvements in reading and spelling followed correction of vision. Though defective vision does not inevitably handicap an individual in spelling—everyone with poor eyesight is not a poor speller—yet it looks as if some specific defects of eyesight rather than the general visual condition does affect spelling. Poor spellers, for example, have frequently been observed to have a small memory span for visually presented material. Spache collected evidence of this from a number of sources, suggesting that limitations in the visual field affected the magnitude of the visual span, and might account for the tendency to perceive in small units.

It has been found that it is possible to increase the span of apprehension to a limited extent by practice and to an impressive extent by the use of a technique such as group-labelling. In this technique, memory span tasks involving random succession of letters in which the longest is 7, can be increased by being grouped into words. Then the sequence can be as long as 20 + letters (Hunter, 1957). Group-labelling is only another name for mnemonic devices, and there are many such that can be exploited in the cause of learning to spell.

In directing the attention of the individual to visual characteristics, we are on much safer ground. There are many reasons for this.

1. Vision is our preferred sense, as humans. If dogs need a frame of reference it would be smell. For humans, to look and see is the way of checking.

2. It is only through visual familiarity with written language that we learn the serial probability of words.

3. It is the words that look alike however they sound which, connected in groups according to their visual pattern, form meaningful connections. The use of mnemonics, i.e. the association with some learned and familiar connection, will reduce the amount to be learned and increase spelling ability as surely as 'group-labelling' has been seen to increase the span of apprehension.

4. Visual learning provides a check. We learn to spell a word. We look to see if it is correct. If it does not 'look right' we learn and check again. This is active self-testing, a most useful ally in every learning situation (Woodworth and Schlosberg, 1955).

No other perceptual avenue provides such a mechanism of verification as 'seeing with your own eyes'.

It is clear, then, that to achieve predictable, infallible and machine-like movements in spelling, we cannot rely on the practice of reading alone to teach us how to spell. We cannot rely on the sound, either heard or imaged, since the alternative spelling possibilities for many syllables make this a very chancy system. Yet *looking* by itself without training in attention to word forms or training in imagery is not enough. Is the answer that we should rely on a multi-sensory approach involving visual, auditory, kinaesthetic and articulatory inroads? Or should we rely on looking, through careful training in the sphere of vision, in, for example, attention, in imagery, and in the learning of probable word patterns and sequences?

These two alternatives suggest the two main ways of teaching spelling. The first is by a sensory amalgam such as Fernald used. She offered a system that would bridge individual differences of sensory preference or habit of imagery. By a system of reinforcement, where finger-tracing concurs with all the other sensory inroads, the child cannot help acquiring the pattern of the words he is learning. He is drilling himself and he is over-learning each word. This is a safe and certain, if lengthy, way. The second is by directing the attention of the individual to the particular characteristics of the word-form.

In the light of these two different but rational approaches to the teaching of spelling, past and current methods of teaching spelling will be reviewed in Chapters 3 and 4, after consideration has been given in the next chapter to what makes for failure or success in this skill.

2

Determinants of competence in spelling

Introduction

What are the main causes of failure in spelling? What makes a person a good speller? Obviously there is no simple answer to these two questions. Some children cannot spell because of some physiological defect; some children cannot spell because they lack the motivation; some children are good spellers because they have had a favourable environment. Order, however, can be introduced into this multiplicity of cause factors by classifying them. Any such classification is bound to be, to a certain extent, arbitrary, but the most convenient one for summarising the main factors that are relevant is to treat them as being those connected with

(1) physical and psychological abilities
(2) educational experiences
(3) motivation.

PHYSICAL AND PSYCHOLOGICAL ABILITIES

(i) *Motor*

The good speller is one for whom, Schonell (1942, 278)

wrote, 'the words flow, as it were from the end of the pen as he thinks of phrases and sentences,' or if you prefer it, one for whom words have become 'engram complexes dependent for their stimuli upon dozens of muscles which have been co-ordinated with definite *strength*, *sequence*, *accuracy* and *rapidity*.' It is inevitable that certain organic defects can prevent such co-ordination and be a major cause of spelling disability. This muscular co-ordination is sometimes difficult to achieve in the case of children with neurological impairment affecting their motor control. Sometimes this is manifested peripherally (though of neurological origin), as in some cerebral-palsied children. For these, the problem may be lack of *strength* and *rapidity*. Sometimes this is central: in such cases this is not merely a question of *strength* and *rapidity*, but of *sequence*, *accuracy* and *direction*. These children, sometimes called 'dyslexic' or 'word-blind' find it very hard to write, but even harder to spell. 'Their handwriting is usually cramped,' writes Roswell Gallagher (1962, 9), 'the letters poorly formed, and the spacing between letters, and the direction in which the letters slant, are variable.' But their spelling is bizarre. They omit, reverse, and confuse letters to such an extent that often it is impossible to guess what they are trying to write. This disability often coincides with difficulty in discriminating right and left, and sometimes with defects of spatial perception, so that not only is there severe motor disability but difficulty in perceptual orientation. Even if these heavily handicapped children could write, they might have difficulty in both perceiving the written word as it is written, and re-organizing it mentally in order to write it.

Such outstanding defects are rare, though less severe disabilities may well affect spelling. 'It is possible,' Abercrombie (1964, 13) writes, 'that the very inability to copy correctly delays the development of perceptual *skills*,' even though the child is well able to perceive what he is trying to copy. Again, in the case of another motor disability, defective speech and faulty pronunciation, Schonell (1934) puts forward considerable evidence that this is a frequent cause of bad spelling, from the early days when young children actually say the words aloud as they write, to the time when there is minimal articulatory movement; and of course poor speech is particularly disastrous for those children who rely over much on auditory recall.

Children who speak distinctly are undoubtedly helped to be good spellers, but some children not only speak distinctly, but are at an even greater advantage in their speech. It has already been argued that the English language being what it is, most people have to select which of two or more alternative vowel combinations to choose in spelling, but for some fortunate children the speech sound itself determines the selection, since they differentiate combinations of vowel sounds in the way they speak! The ones who enjoy this advantage are the Scots, for the Scottish dialect, stemming from Northumbria, retains the purity of the Anglo-Saxon vowels. There are, of course, many variations of accent, some 'purer' than others. But all Scots to some extent expose the diphthong in the way they pronounce the word, so that they pronounce 'played' in a low and long tone, while 'plaid' is pronounced high with the diphthong sounded. The writer could not understand why there were more homophone errors (words that sound alike but look different) amongst i.t.a. taught children she tested, than Livingston (1961) found in her Scottish *Study of Spelling Errors*, until it was pointed out that Scottish children differentiate homophones orally. 'Tide' is long and low, but 'tied' is high with a diphthong. Again the Scots are conscious of, and differentiate between the internal vowel; *fur* and *fir* are not pronounced the same, nor are *turn* and *tern*. In fact in some areas the 'ight' in 'might' could not lead to confusion with 'mite'. There is no excuse for poor spelling on the grounds of slovenliness of speech among the Scots.

(ii) *Sensation*

The second and, one would think, the most likely area to contribute to poor spelling is that involving the senses.

(a) *Hearing:* It might be expected that children with poor hearing might be handicapped in spelling. But this is not so. Comparing the spelling of deaf children with normal children of the same reading ability, the deaf children were found to be superior by three or four years (Gates and Chase, 1926). Templin, too, in 1954 found that both deaf and hard of hearing children made substantially fewer errors than 'hearing' children in theme writing. It is probable that these children relied almost exclusively on the visual pattern of word structure as they wrote, since by definition they were unable to differentiate small auditory differences, and English, as has been demonstrated at length, demands awareness of visual rather than auditory patterns.

(b) *Sight:* Even more, in the light of emphasis placed throughout this monograph on the importance of looking, it might be expected that children with poor sight might be handicapped in spelling. Apart from the inevitable handicaps and their repercussions on spelling experienced by the partially sighted, children who have to wear glasses and yet are within the range of normality, spell as well as those who do not. It is not acuity of vision that distinguishes the good spellers from the bad (Russell, 1937).

It is possible that if the visual field is limited for some reason, the child, like a horse in blinkers, sees only a small area at a time. This could explain the smaller visual memory span often found in poor spellers (Spache, 1940c). It does not look, however, as if the acuity of vision, which makes a child able to discriminate visually between letters, is a cause of inability to spell as much as it is an earlier cause of inability to read. Even in reading, isolated sensory deficiencies have hardly ever been shown to be insurmountable handicaps (Fendrick, 1935).

With normal children spelling ability is not so much affected by slight peripheral disabilities as by central difficulties (Hartmann, 1931). In other words it is not the eyes and the ears but what goes on behind them that really affects spelling, the perceptual rather than the sensory mechanisms.

(iii) *Perception*

It is important at the outset to distinguish between neural impairment which is very readily confused with sensory disability. The child's ears and eyes may be efficient but the child still cannot hear or see. What looks like perceptual disability may of course be habitual lack of attention, for severe neural impairment of the kind that would inevitably affect reading and spelling is rare.

There seems to be, however, one aspect of the perceptual process that really does affect spelling. Hartmann (1931) spoke of it as a particular 'form of looking', which was quite distinct from any specific sensory ability or facility in integrating such sensory abilities.

Let us consider what is meant by this particular 'form of looking'. Although the small span of visual apprehension found in poor spellers can be associated with a visual field limited optically, in the retina itself, it is what goes on when a child reproduces a word from a flash card that is interesting in this connection. Good spellers perceive total configurations or, one might say, see the word as a whole more easily than poor spellers (Hartmann, 1931). Now we work on the assumption that perceptual disabilities can be com-

pensated for in training and we know that the more familiar words are, the more likely we are to see them as a
whole (Howes and Solomon, 1951). So this may well be a
means of training this perception of wholes, by teaching
the child to spell words already familiar to him. It is a
strong justification for the infant school practice of 'catching words' (see page 43) and of making a start at learning
the word as a whole when written in his personal dictionary by the teacher, and not blindly copying (see page 50).
The need to look at words as wholes has been repeatedly
observed. As early as 1923, Hilderbrandt suggested that, in
learning to spell, it was unwise to lay too much stress on
phonic elements, as these might well obstruct the view of
the word as a sequence of significant parts or as a whole.
Again in 1936 Higley and Higley recommended that, in
learning to spell a word, a child should, in the first instance,
just look at the word without saying, spelling or writing it,
as these intrusions might confuse his learning.

'Looking at a word as a whole' is a vague term which has
been heavily and justifiably criticized by supporters of
phonic reading schemes (e.g. Diack, 1960). What this
phrase means, in terms of spelling needs, is that the word
must be reproducible when exposed for a short time on a
tachistoscope or a flash card. For this the word must be
either familiar (in terms of reading experiences) or short
enough to be within the individual's span of apprehension
for unconnected elements. The more familiar the word, the
longer it can be. Presumably a word that is familiar to a
child in the process of his reading, when exposed on a flash
card, is not merely reproduced in a memory image, but
recognized as in reading and then in recall *built up into its
component parts*. The word is not recalled but remade in
the light of the child's reading experience with this particular word. It might have been thought that this would not
help in dealing with unfamiliar words; hence the preoccu-

pation of teachers with syllabication, with marking hard spots etc. But reproducing the word correctly, when it is both new and long, depends on first being able to read it, and then in the light of experience with groups of letters that go together (the old 'sequential probability'), being able to reconstruct the word in plausible forms.

If, on the other hand, we do not limit the time of exposure of a word, by tachistoscope or flash card, but give the child time to study a word he is to spell, his eyes move about the word, lighting on different parts for varying lengths of time and going back over parts again. From looking at such eye-movements it is known that good spellers make fewer and shorter fixations than poor spellers, see more of the word at a time, and make fewer regressive movements. Younger and less mature children are also less efficient in eye-movements than older children, (Gilbert and Gilbert, 1942).

Inefficiency of eye-movements is a perceptual habit which is not a cause of but a concomitant of poor spelling. Gilbert and Gilbert (1942) put the cause of this in poor study habits, over-emphasis and overstudy, thoroughness rather than efficiency. Gilbert's study techniques to overcome this will be described in a later chapter.

(iv) *Imagery*

There is no doubt that imagery is of very great importance in spelling. Grey Walter has suggested (1964) that certain brain rhythms and certain forms of imagery go together. This may well imply that there is initially an organic structural basis to imagery. Yet there is no question that imagery changes its mode as we develop. This is particularly so in the case of abstract thinkers. It is possible that our preferred form of imagery develops, as we mature, from a more generalized system which may or may not have stronger emphases, visual, auditory, kinaesthetic. We certainly rely on imagery in spelling, and probably to greater advantage if we rely on visual imagery. This fortunately can be trained.

Given two weeks' training Radaker (1963) found that after one year the imagery trained groups scored significantly higher on spelling tests than did the control group, showing that visual imagery is successful in improving spelling performance over longer periods of time. As a corollary he adds that the improvement in spelling suggests that it will also be effective in reading because of the effort devoted to word recognition and recall.

EDUCATIONAL EXPERIENCES

Though there is some correlation between spelling ability and reading attainment (e.g. Townsend, 1947), most poor readers being also poor spellers, spelling failure is widely distributed throughout the range of ability (Russell, 1937) and personality (Holmes, 1959). It is reasonable, then, to look at extrinsic causation of failure to spell. Indeed Schonell, in his classic research into factors contributing to spelling achievement attributed the chief influence to school experiences.

When Gordon gave tests to gypsies, who made only a third of the attendances at school of normal children, and canal boat children, who made only a twentieth of the attendance of ordinary children, he found that over the range of school subjects these children were most backward in spelling. Missing school seemed to be a very great handicap to these children in learning to spell. This is plausible. Children deprived of school life for any reason are bombarded with invitations to read—the daily newspaper, advertisements on hoardings or transport and most of all on commercial television. They have a very strong incentive to manipulate their money adequately, but there are few occasions when children need to write—particularly children in a less literate social group. This is supported by Norris (1940) who showed that the standards of 14-15-year-olds who were still at school, tended to be higher in spelling than that of young adults, and that spelling ability was maintained or improved only in the more able who continue to practise their skills. The average pupil tended to decline appreciably by 18 and the more backward ones more rapidly. Indeed the lowest 10% of pupils who approximated at best to eleven-year-old spelling dropped back to an eight-year-old level some four years later. Reading comprehension, by contrast, seems to go on improving since the great majority do practise some sort of reading in daily life.

(i) *Opportunity to write creatively*

The case for children learning to spell through creative writing is based on our awareness of individual differences. Some children write fluently and at length, some deliberately and unadventurously. The variety of attack and of style reflects the differences in the number and kind of 'asked for' words. These differences will determine the breadth of correct spelling vocabulary which a child will possess by the end of the Junior School, however much it has been supplemented by the teaching of suitable lists and the learning of associative clues to groups of words together with the rationale of certain spelling rules and how these are to be applied.

There will still be individual differences in spelling achievement, and these will presumably depend on the extent to which incidental learning has also taken place. As Hildreth (1956, 34) says, 'the amount of successful incidental learning a child will do depends largely upon the challenge his environment offers him and the interests he discovers for himself in the situations that confront him.' The child who has needed to write, or has been challenged and inveigled into writing, is likely to be a better speller than one who escapes with a few desultory paragraphs about 'a rainy day'. It is probable that the child who has savoured words, and as the metaphor suggests, enjoyed, mouthed and articulated them will become more aware of their structure. His enjoyment of words may well stem from good teaching, from stories he has heard with repetitions that he has been able to join in and chant, from interchange of conversation with a teacher or parent, from the opportunity to express an activity in words. Such opportunity is evident in the case of the four-year-old who picked up sticky papers saying, 'sticky, sticky, sloshy', or the five-year-old who can write in his book, 'One day I can see in my head there is a witch. It is horrid,' and a week later, 'Boots boots nothing but boots, boots, yes boots, no boots, yes boots, no boots, boots can wait to be put on, the boots wait and wait.' Or another in the same class who wrote, 'Daddy made a cupboard and my brother painted the cupboard with Bovril so Mummy had to wipe it up again and Daddy put the doors on the next day and Daddy put the catches on the doors on the cupboard.' But this is all speculative. There is no evidence at present that these verbal experiences produce superior spellers. Indeed the evidence of one experiment by the writer to investigate the effects of different reading methods on free writing showed that though there were statistically significant differences in the quality of writing, there was no difference between the two groups in spelling attainment. This was presumably because the children were all writing *without guidance* as to how to attempt to spell successfully. They were not instructed in dictionary techniques of any kind and there was no encouragement to learn the words the children were feeling the need to spell. Amongst more vividly writing children one can expect a fanning upwards of writing experience, and it is possible that under proper guidance in learning to spell the words they want to write the children who make a more adventurous choice of words and evolve more divergent plots will, by positive reinforcement, gain greater awareness of the structure of English spelling.

(ii) *Early perceptual experiences*

The earliest point at which children become aware that words can be 'drawn' or as we should say 'coded' on paper, is when they look at the book as their mother reads to them. They may well sit and 'read' the book upside down, but soon will follow a familiar story from picture to picture and page to page. Left-right eye movements are developing. It is plausible to hazard that this satisfying activity has some effect on the child's later attitude to words and perhaps even to spelling, at least in the urge to write and to ask for more daring and exciting words to be spelt.

But when such 'learning' to read in the pre-school years gives place to being 'taught' to read, perceptual techniques that are no longer haphazard are laid down. Children are not only incidentally but often deliberately taught, in pre-reading activities, left to right eye movements. Children taught by the Look and Say method are presented with a few carefully chosen words and implicitly encouraged to recognize words by the ups and downs of the word patterns, by length of words, by initial or final letters—in other words by visual recognition. Children taught by the Phonic method are taught to analyse letter by letter, and later, as they acquire the phonic code, phoneme by phoneme, before synthesis into meaningful words. But children are not only implicitly encouraged in these perceptual techniques but explicitly directed, drilled and reinforced.

It seems reasonable that a skill such as spelling which depends so much on perceptual habits, might, in part at least, spring from perceptual techniques of this kind acquired at critical learning periods. The hypothesis that there is transfer from such perceptual drills, exercises and habits to the mechanisms of spelling has been explored. Experiments were set up by the writer to investigate the different effects of specific reading methods. In an experiment comparing the spelling of 138 eight-year-old children taught to read by rigorous Look and Say and Phonic methods, there was found to be no difference in the overall spelling attainment of children taught by either method. Nor was there any difference when comparing the spelling attainment in another experiment involving 230 children taught to read in the medium of i.t.a. and traditional orthography. Nevertheless very interesting qualitative differences in the spelling of these three groups appeared when the errors in a diagnostic dictation were analysed. The error categories used were the traditional ones (Masters, 1927; Spache, 1940a and b; Livingston, 1961) except in the case of 'substitution with reasonable phonic alternatives' and 'substitutions of phonic alternatives not conforming to rule'. These categories were included as it seemed possible that here might appear the effect of training in reading. And so it did.

In the experiment comparing the spelling of children taught by a Look and Say method and those taught by a Phonic method, it was found that the greatest error difference occurred in just these 'reasonable phonic alternatives', the Phonic group making significantly more 'reasonable phonic alternatives' than the Look and Say group ($p = <\cdot01$). On the other hand the Phonic group made significantly less unclassifiable errors than the Look and Say group ($p = <\cdot01$).

Comparing the spelling of children taught in the two media, i.t.a. and t.o., though again there was no difference in spelling attainment, the analysis of errors revealed very different profiles. Children taught by the initial teaching alphabet made significantly (p=<·001) more errors in the single for double letter error. They wrote, for example, 'troting' for 'trotting', and 'trafic' for 'traffic'. They made significantly more reasonable phonic alternatives e.g. 'shood' for 'should' and 'rane' for 'rain'. They made significantly more homophones, 'tide' for 'tied', and 'herd' for 'heard' (p=<·001). Children taught in traditional orthography made significantly more errors suggesting faulty auditory perception or encoding, perseveration and unclassified errors. In other words, children taught in i.t.a. spell more economically (writing no more letters than is strictly necessary) yet make more errors of judgement, making the wrong choice in the matter of doubling, substitution of consonants, homophones and phonic alternatives not conforming to precedent, presumably because these children are as yet inexperienced in the serial probability of words.

When the methods and media are ranked according to the percentage of errors in each category an interesting trend emerges. It is seen that i.t.a. produces fewest of the kind of errors that arise from lack of economy and control of output, namely omissions, insertions, and perseverations. The Look and Say method produces better visual attack with fewest doubling errors, consonant substitutions, nonconforming phonic alternatives, errors of faulty auditory perception, and homophones resulting in consonantal exactness, accuracy of overall structuring and superior semantic association. Between this and the economy and discipline of i.t.a. at the other end of the continuum, lies the phonic method, neither fewest nor most in any of the above categories, yet superior in the remaining ones of fewest transpositions, fewest substitutions of vowels and the greatest number of reasonable phonic alternatives. So the two reading methods, Look and Say, and Phonic, and the use of the Initial Teaching Alphabet, when rigorously and unexceptionally operated, do not seem to affect the level of spelling attainment. On the other hand, it does seem as if the perceptual training involved in the different reading methods is transferred to spelling techniques. Here indeed is an example of the effect of educational experiences on spelling.

It is interesting to speculate on the future spelling ability of children who rely on visual reference, as the Look and Say group do, or follow a more rational, rule-following procedure, as Phonic and i.t.a taught children do, especially in a language which is only partly regular. No doubt individual differences in many particulars exploit or nullify the advantages inherent in such particular forms of reference that stem from particular reading methods. The combinations are legion, but their effect on spelling indisputable.

(iii) *Spelling teaching*

If early perceptual training in learning to read has such an effect on later spelling, it is to be expected that the training given in spelling lessons has as great, if not greater, influence. It will be shown in Chapter 3 that children left to themselves with word-lists 'learn' these in a very haphazard kind of way, reciting alphabetically, reading over the words, etc., and that the time spent on spelling can be used more effectively if children are taught to attend carefully to word-structure, to look for the 'hard spots', to identify familiar word sequences within long words, to syllabize, to exercise visual imagery. It will also be shown in Chapter 3 that children can be encouraged to attend to the visual structure of unknown words that are needed in the course of creative writing.

We may ask how autonomous are the children in their

learning to spell the words they need. How ego-involved are they in their learning to spell correctly? Do they write out their corrections intelligently or do they copy them blindly? The answer must be, surely, that much of their attitude to spelling must stem from school practices, from habits of autonomy and involvement in the learning process, in other words from extrinsic causation.

MOTIVATIONAL

(i) *A casual attitude generally*

But however autonomous children are trained to be in learning to spell, however high a standard of hand-writing, punctuation etc. is set, so that to give in an untidy and careless piece of work is against the class-room norm, there are still some children, like adults, who seem to present a casual attitude generally. It is evident in many overt ways, in appearance, in stance, in writing, in speech, in work, and not least in their attention to details of word structure. In his research on 'Personality and Spelling Ability' Holmes (1959) showed that only a small area of spelling success could be attributed to personality factors. His conclusions suggest a relationship between good spelling ability and the tendency to be individualistic, anti-social, and less gregarious, but more intellectually efficient, analytic, composed, confident and critical in thinking. The worst spellers, it seems, tend to be undependable, irresponsible, impulsive, defiant, tactless, improvident, to show an inability to calculate their own social stimulus value, but apparently to accept life as something to be enjoyed!

(ii) *The self-image*

It is probably only when children are motivated to pay attention to the structures of a word, to retain the perception, to overlearn, to follow practices of active self-testing, to produce with pride a well-presented piece of work that they are going to become good spellers. Motivation at such a rigorous level depends not on externally imposed incentives of immediate rewards (the prize) or long term (success, advancement, status), not on the desire to conform, to communicate courteously, but on the self-image the individual has of himself as a good speller. Prescott Lecky (1945) turns to spelling as exemplifying human self-consistency. He quotes the intelligent poor speller, tutored ineffectively, his deficiency not due to lack of ability but to an active resistance which prevents him from learning how to spell in spite of extra instruction. 'The resistance arises from the fact that at some time in the past the suggestion that he is a poor speller was accepted and incorporated into his definition of himself, and is now an integral part of his total personality.' He must conform to this standard, must be 'true to himself'. 'If he defines himself as a poor speller', Lecky writes (p. 104), 'the misspelling of a certain proportion of the words which he uses becomes for him a moral issue. He misspells words for the same reason that he refuses to be a thief. That is, he must endeavour to behave in a manner consistent with his conception of himself'.

Such poor spellers maintain their standard of poor spelling. There is approximately the same number of errors on each page, yet, as Lecky points out, the spelling of a foreign language seems to be unimpaired, showing that the difficulty cannot be attributed to eye-movements, left-handedness or other mechanical interferences. In such cases the clinical technique which Lecky suggests, is to find strong values apparently unrelated to, in this case, spelling, which the student emulates, but which are inconsistent with poor spelling. For example, the student may like to think of himself as independent and self-reliant; yet the poor speller expects his defect to be condoned and treated indulgently.

If the student can see the inconsistency here, Lecky suggests he will reject his definition of himself as a poor speller and determine to establish the opposite definition.

The moral for teachers is, of course, that, at all costs, children should be prevented from developing a self-image of themselves as bad spellers. In Mathematics, it is hoped, we are approaching the point when girls will no longer 'have blind spots about Maths'. We are approaching Mathematics via the exploration of order and relationships in the environment. Such orderings and relationships are to be observed and experienced, not presented as a challenge in the form of sums to the child who is inexperienced and insecure in manipulating figures, and who, getting them wrong repeatedly, is led to conclude 'I'm no good at it', so that this definition is laid down permanently. In the same way the child whose composition book or diary is fiercely corrected with red pencil, who experiences the insecurity of inadequate visual or rational reference, who is told to try first, but knows he will get it wrong, concludes 'I'm no good at spelling' and again his definition of himself is laid down and he proceeds to live up to it.

For this reason, many teachers do not correct errors in compositions in red pencil. Some rub out the error and let the child fill in the correct version from memory. For this reason, many present a system of reference, personal dictionaries or requests to the teacher, simple printed dictionaries, or lists of common words displayed. Words that have been written correctly are learned efficiently and economically with positive reinforcement. So methods of teaching both reading and spelling are designed to combine the best of all worlds, so that children can use visual reference, ('Lemme write it down and see if it's right') possess some rational reference, so that, if they make an error, it is a logical and hence remediable one, and mnemonic, so that they gradually connect words that are visually similar with common words that are keys to less usual words.

Children who already possess this unfortunate self-image need the kind of clinical technique Lecky suggests for older people. They must be brought to see the inconsistency between themselves as independent or efficient, or precise, or courteous, and as poor spellers, re-defining themselves in terms not compatible with themselves as poor spellers. It is vital that children should never acquire a self-image of themselves as poor spellers, and to this end all possible help in the way of word-study and of visual and rational reference should be provided.

3

Traditional approaches to the teaching of spelling

What to learn

The two approaches to the teaching of spelling suggested at the end of Chapter 1 are concerned with how rather than with what to teach. The 'How' has been a much more sophisticated concern in the history of education, than the 'what'. So first we will return to the 'what' which has indeed been a major preoccupation with research workers in spelling.

Long before the incidental learning controversy (which is very much a 'how' question) teachers were concerned with what words children should learn and they were making word lists to this end. One dated 1882, but found in a primary school cupboard in the 1950's, includes in one lesson the words, 'bissextile', 'decennial', 'chimerical', and 'chalybeate'! Such lists are obviously not derived from children's language either spoken or written. Indeed it was not until 1911 that words ceased to be selected arbitrarily and were selected on the basis of the frequency with which they occurred. In that year Eldridge recorded the 60,000 most common English words from newspapers. In the next few years counts were made particularly of the spelling vocabulary of personal and business letters (Ayres, 1913) because here spelling deficiency was most embarrassingly revealed. The following year the first list derived from children's writing (Cook and O'Shea, 1914) appeared. This has been succeeded through the years by many counts taken from children's writing of compositions and letters, culminating in the recent word count of children's writing by Edwards and Gibbons in their Leicestershire Vocabulary Survey which, though designed to help writers and publishers of books for the youngest readers, is an indication of the words children write, not necessarily what they want to write.

Since counts of words used by children in their own writing are the most real evidence of what children want to write, it is obviously on these that the spelling lists should be based. Not many, however, are based directly on children's writing. One of the most extensive and thorough is that by Rinsland (1945), who examined and graded more than six million words in 100,000 scripts of children, from 416 American cities. The resulting spelling list contained only words appearing more than three times in any one grade. This list was further graded by Hildreth (1953) who noted how words became so highly specialized after the first 2,000 or so that it was difficult to determine which to include in primary school spelling lists. Johnson's list (1950) from children's writing was confined to the hundred words he found that children in their writing were most likely to mis-spell. In 1955, the Scottish Council for Research in Education took a much more positive line by producing a spelling vocabulary, derived from a count of the words in 70,000 compositions written freely by 7-12-year-old pupils in Scottish schools, on topics selected to suit their interests.

Many lists, however, have been prepared, often subjectively, from other sources, often remote from children's writing needs, from e.g. adults' correspondence or adults'

37

reading material, as was the famous 30,000 word list of Thorndike and Lorge (1944). To do this is to teach children to spell words that adults, not they themselves, write. No wonder Fernald wrote 'Formal word lists will always fail to supply the particular word a person should learn at a particular time' (1943, 210). Words which children are learning from derived lists may well be the words they will not need till they themselves are adult and writing formal letters; for it has been found that there is little in common between the vocabulary of children's writing and that of adults' formal literary writing. Hildreth confirmed earlier findings that derived spelling word lists were very different in content from the words used in children's writing She also found that word forms that children use may be different from the forms appearing in derived lists e.g. children make more frequent use of the past tense and of the plural form than the present tense and singular form that appear in the lists.

If a list is derived it is important to know its source. Apart from those already mentioned as having stemmed from word counts of children's writing, most spelling lists have been derived from word counts, particularly from Thorndike's. Washburne's spelling curriculum (1923) was based partly on Thorndike's lists, though in part on adult correspondence and children's compositions. Breed (1930) answered, 'What words should children be taught to spell?' from sixteen different sources, eleven of which were adult. Even Schonell's familiar 'Essential Spelling List' (1932), the one most widely used in English schools, is a subjective list derived from Horn (adults' writing, 1926) and Thorndike (adults' reading material, 1921), though here there is an empirically based relationship with well standardized norms of spelling ability, i.e. with what children can, not necessarily with what they want to spell.

Gates' (1937) list was derived from a count of words in

twenty-five spelling books used in American schools. Bixler (1940) produced a standard spelling scale from eight sources and thus to the popular *Keywords to Literacy* (1962), a derived list, but one intended as a minimum sight vocabulary to be used in the teaching of reading and not primarily intended as a spelling list.

From such lists, the Bureau of Curriculum Research of the Board of Education in the City of New York compiled a list of 5,000 words graded into ten frequency levels. From this State list, the New Zealand Council of Educational Research list of 2,700 words was originally derived (1960). But this was only a starting point. This list was widely examined by inspectors, college lecturers and teachers. and checked against a number of well-known derived lists as well as word counts of New Zealand children's writing. By so checking, the faults and omissions of a derived list have been ironed out and the resulting list is almost certainly the most adequate in use today.

How to learn

Many spelling books have been produced with lists devised in devious ways, but few until recently said much about how to set about learning. Students presented with nonsense words to learn to spell, soon find it necessary to evolve an efficient method. Most students depend on associative clues and mnemonics; rarely do they depend on rote learning. Must children, inexperienced in organization of material to be learned and unaware of the laws of learning, be expected to evolve by trial and error an economical method of learning spelling lists?

Learning to spell, without being given instructions as to how to learn, leads to haphazard techniques which may well be inappropriate to a particular child's idiosyncrasies of perception and imagery. It may, for example, lead children to spell alphabetically. This is a time-honoured method, but it involves an unnecessarily complicated sequence of events. The child learns the word by reading it and repeating the alphabetic names of the letters. He writes it by first saying the name of each letter in turn and writing it before reading the completed word. He is using two distinct codes, the alphabetic name code and the 'sounds', and one does not immediately evoke the other. If we hear a word spelt by alphabetic letter names, the word is not immediately meaningful. We have to translate the names into sounds. If the word is spelt by sounds, long before it is finished, we have leapt mentally, with immediacy of perception, to complete the whole word with almost certainly a visual, and probably an auditory image, concomitant with the meaning of the word. This is only one example of the precariousness of leaving children to learn uninstructed by trial and error.

Fulton pointed out in 1914, in the days when spelling lists of dubious origin and derivation abounded, that pupils following a systematic method make much greater progress and retain their learning better than those given no directions for learning to spell. Twenty years later Alice Watson (1935) was recommending that children should be taught to master efficient techniques for self-teaching. Only too often children, given a list without a method, read over the list rapidly or recite the names of the letters, names that have no immediate relation to the overall sound of the word. A somewhat more sophisticated way of learning is to learn syllabically, sounding the syllables one by one. But to rely wholly on auditory memory is to put oneself in a position of uncertainty when faced with the alternatives presented by even regular phonemic words, and it is a pity to rely on a method that breaks down just when it is most needed. Unsupported by other sensory inroads, this is a precarious means to spelling.

Schonell (1942), of course, pointed out that the visual, auditory and articulatory elements must be 'firmly cemented by writing'. For by writing the attention is focussed and 'helps to bridge the gap between visual and auditory symbols by successive production of the constituent parts of the visual form.' This writing which gives children the 'feel' of the word is vital to correct spelling. As children progress they become less and less aware of the visual, auditory, and articulatory elements, until they achieve the machine-like movement where, as they write, the initial letter initiates the muscular contraction stimulating the second letter in a chain-like series, a chain reaction supplying the whole word. There is such a moment in learning to type when, instead of typing letter by letter, the student suddenly in one sweep produces a word. T-h-e is produced in one satisfying, complete unalterable movement. The first letter, t, triggers off the h, the h, the e, and if the typist images the word it may well be in muscular contractions in the three fingers involved. It is here that the teacher of typing restrains the student, in the enthusiasm of his new found skill, from typing each word with a flourish, and stopping at the end of each word. In the interests of using the typewriter efficiently, he then attends to the phrase, sentence and paragraph rather than word wholes. The *gestalt* is enlarged and this is achieved by the teacher's insistence on rhythmical typing. It is interesting, incidentally, to speculate on the possible effect on spelling of this insistence on rhythmic technique.

Repeated writing, however much it bridges the gap between visual and auditory symbols, involves auditory and articulatory elements only implicitly. Schonell spoke of 'the absolute necessity of emphasizing with backward spellers all means of ingress in learning words, the visual, the auditory and the kinaesthetic'. A child or adult may be handicapped by one rather weak sensory mechanism; he may have poor perceptual grasp of the significance of a word, his imagery may be very one-sided or he may be distracted by other sensory stimuli. If such a child is bombarded by several sensory stimuli supporting each other in emphasizing the structure of a word to remember, he will inevitably attend to and learn the word. And this is what Fernald suggests (1943): an amalgam of the sensory input. Sight, of course, is being translated from receptor into effector finger movements and pencil movements, but it is supplemented by simultaneous oral articulation of the word, the hearing of this slowly spoken word, together with the tactile sensation as the child traces with his bare forefinger the word he is learning. Each child possesses an office file and inserts the word he needs alphabetically, after he has finger-traced it often enough for him to be able to write it correctly in his composition. Much later we find him, faced with a new word, finger-tracing unobtrusively on the desk or on his knee! Often the more sophisticated learner of spelling not only articulates the word subvocally as he writes, but makes slight head or finger movements, long after he has abandoned a finger-tracing technique, an overt sign of the retention of the oral and kinaesthetic imagery he initiated when learning by finger-tracing. All possible perceptual channels are left open. Children can learn, in spite of their individual differences, without recourse to complicated and tedious investigation by the teacher to find the best method for any particular child to pursue.

The Gates-Russell diagnostic test (1940) is one such elaborate and lengthy type of investigation, revealing the most congenial method a particular child employs in spelling with a view to exploiting the child's habits, strengths and facility. The test will be described in Chapter 5. 'Spelling disability', they write (p. 41), 'is usually a highly individual matter,' and they are eclectic in their approach to the remedial teaching of spelling. They advocate individual and independent methods of word-study (attention to hard spots, pointing out familiar word forms in longer words, syllabizing, visualizing, hearing, pronouncing the word, spelling it orally, and writing it) and this repeatedly in different situations. They stress the motivational aspect, changed attitudes to spelling and changed habits, for example, of verifying doubtful words. In such an unphonemic language as English they point out the importance of good visual techniques. Children should work on their own errors as well as on lists, and devices unrelated to spelling are of less use than intrinsic functional practice materials, emphasizing context spelling rather than words in isolation.

This, though an eclectic programme for individuals, is an all-embracing programme including both the multi-sensory approach as advocated by Fernald for universal use and the word-study approach. Techniques such as Fernald's are applicable at any stage of school learning. Supplementary techniques to improve attention to word-structure are needed in the early stages, and in the remedial or lower streams of the Secondary Modern School.

It is probably sufficient in the Infant School to provide the simple kind of technique practised by many good Infant teachers (Luke, 1931). There is a game of 'catching' and writing words from flash cards, perhaps a step or two behind the words the children are learning to read. (This is incidentally an excellent training in *looking* and remembering words as wholes, and one we could well emulate with older children.) It must be noted here that some duller children of all ages find it very difficult to write a word of which they know the meaning, the sound, and which they can recognize at sight. Some of these children seem to need to go through a preparatory stage of writing down the letters, sound by sound, before they can easily learn the look of a word. This can be practised with the three-letter words in the first group of the Schonell Essential list, but it is probably best acquired in free writing by finger-tracing in the manner advocated by Fernald.

Lists without suggested techniques

A number of spelling books have been published in the last few years fulfilling various functions. Some still present lists of words to be learned without any indication of how to learn. In some, such as *Spelling* by John Smith (1961), this is deliberate. Words are grouped according to structure, and children find the word that fits the definition and write it down, presumably copying it, but the internal structure will have been noted. The children are not told how to learn these, in fact they are not told to learn them at all. Their object is the search for a word, and it is very probable that, provided, as in this case, attention is centred on the structure of a word, spelling is more easily acquired when the object is something other than just learning to spell. After all, the motivation is stronger in searching for a word and completing a whole.

Lists with suggested techniques

The spelling lists with the most explicit technical instructions as to how to learn are those in the *Alphabetical Spelling List* prepared and published by the New Zealand Council for Educational Research. The first English edition was published in 1963. It consists of an alphabetical list of words, as has already been described, derived from the New York State list.

The frequency levels of the chosen words are indicated for each of the words, so that children can see for themselves how relatively probable it is that the words they are learning will be needed by them. This at once indicates the degree of autonomy expected of the children in this field.

A child is expected to compile a personal learning list and if words entered are from a lower level than his current working level, these should be underlined, thus providing automatic revision. 'The child,' says Arvidson (1963, 20), 'should be encouraged to adopt a particularly determined attitude towards words that persistently give him trouble.' Again the onus is on the child in this learning situation.

The dictionary form of the spelling list demands dictionary skills, to isolate the first and later the second and third letters of a word, to have some idea of the part of the dictionary to open, and the need to range forward and backward till the word is found. When it is found, specific instructions are given to copy the word. In the later learning period, the child is given instructions as to how to learn to spell, by writing, looking, saying, listening, saying again, finger-tracing on the desk and saying as he writes. He is instructed to cover and write from memory with his finger, and later to write with a pencil and check.

These are specific instructions, for a systematic procedure. It is assumed that the children work autonomously, independently and responsibly. They are instructions to children to use a number of 'perceptual paths into the memory', visual, auditory, kinaesthetic, followed by testing, overlearning and revision.

Arvidson reminds us of individual differences in learning methods and recommends that the weaker spellers should be studied and helped to find their best techniques. But instructions accompanying the word lists are systematic generalized instructions for class use.

Teaching of spelling by rules

Now some children can approach spelling from a much more rational angle than others, and grasp and apply rules earlier and more efficiently than others. Most rules taught come from the teachers' experience, only a few from text-books. Here the great difficulty is in the wording of the rules, for example, 'Words ending in silent "e" drop the "e" when adding a suffix beginning with a vowel, and keep the "e" when adding a suffix beginning with a consonant.' This is the first of four rules framed by Wheat (1932, 700) and one which he said was short, simple, easy to learn, remember and use, and had the advantage of covering 23% of the words in the vocabulary he analysed with less than 1% exception. Another rule ran (page 703) 'monosyllables and words of more than one syllable with the accent on the last syllable, which end in a single consonant preceded by a single vowel, double the final consonant when adding a suffix beginning with a vowel.' The length and technical-ity of such rules are frightening, yet we are reminded that, by the time the child needs to spell untaught words, he can comprehend and use such rules. This is very question-able since use of technical terms, e.g. noun, plural, singular, suffix, etc. presupposes a mental level far in advance of the *use* of nouns, plurals, singulars.

It is generally agreed that:

(a) The rule must apply to a large number of words.
(b) It must have few exceptions.
(c) The statement of the rules must be simple and easily comprehended while being sufficiently exact to cover only the appropriate words.

'Before a new rule is introduced,' writes McLeod (1961, 130), 'the following should be borne in mind. Knowledge of a rule serves no useful purpose unless it covers a number of words which might reasonably be expected to be already in the children's spelling vocabulary and embraces also other words likely to be needed which the children may spell by generalization.' No wonder Vallins (1965, 15) writes

'There are no reliable rules and even the guiding principles of which there are more than we imagine, are apt sometimes to fail and mislead both ear and eye.' McLeod's own research showed that presenting each word separately was a better method than teaching words with the aid of spelling rules where applicable. As Foran (1934, 141) said, 'If a rule involves unfamiliar terms, it may become a major difficulty in itself and contribute nothing to spelling.'

Test-study plan, rather than Study-test method

Fernald, as we have seen, maintained that the most satisfactory spelling vocabulary is that supplied by the child himself. She condemns spelling books and word lists as never supplying the particular word a writer requires at a specific moment. But there is another difficulty about spelling lists in the economy of time and effort for the child. Most spelling lists, both with and without instructions as to how to learn the words, imply 'These words must be learned at a particular stage.' But some of the words will be already known by the children. Some words will be more easily learnt and with less attention on the part of a child than others. There is a 'curve of mastery' for each word. Some children learn a particular word early, some late, some easily, some with difficulty. And, as we have seen, there is considerable progress in learning to spell incidentally from year to year apart from practice in spelling lessons. In fact, Thompson (1930) found that many words are known before they are studied. Of 2,127 words, 25% were spelled correctly before study by 84% children. It is reasonable then, in presenting a spelling list, for these words to be tested before being learned (Gates, 1931), so that for children, who can already spell some of the words, time is not wasted, effort misdirected, and early success not enjoyed.

If lists are to be learned it would seem economical for the practice suggested by Bernard (1931) and quoted in the Scottish *Studies in Spelling* (1961), to be followed. Children knowing the number of words to be learned should work in pairs, testing each other and learning the required number of words from the series of lists. This is the Test-study in contrast to the traditional study-test method. The fact that the writer has not found this in use in any of the schools being studied suggests that this is either a very unwieldy method or that its justification and value are not appreciated.

4

Current approaches to the teaching of spelling

Creative writing and drill

In the last chapter it became clear that spelling lists were not enough unless supplemented by careful and systematic instructions as to how to learn the words in the lists. It may have been observed that the most detailed and probably the most effective instructions were those devised by Fernald and by Arvidson in the cause of, and for use in, the course of children's free writing. Fernald was certainly not satisfied with the mere learning of arbitrary lists which probably have not supplied the words the child requires. 'The most satisfactory spelling vocabulary is that supplied by the child himself.' We are reminded by Hildreth of the close relationship between growth in language and progress in spelling, and that spelling is learned by constant practice in writing.

Yet ability in spelling cannot be acquired by just writing —as well we know from the creative writing of young children. Some method must be found whereby children can with the least possible withdrawal of attention from their creative writing be faced with the correct spelling of the word they need.

Class dictionaries, but more often individual dictionaries, are used in schools to satisfy this need. A child asks for a word and it is written in his individual dictionary. He copies it into his free writing and continues to write. There is a speedy return to the child's creative work, but no sooner has the word been written in the composition, than the word is, as it were, wiped out mentally, in the same way that we look up a telephone number, dial the number and wipe out the number so effectively that if we are given a wrong number, we have to look up the number again in the directory. In the same way, a child, having written the word and wiped out the memory of it, may forget it to the point of asking the teacher for that same word again the same day. It is necessary, therefore, to *direct* the child's attention to the word that has been written, and to insist on his writing it in his composition, as a whole, from memory. Surely this is the essence of Fernald's technique. For normally-learning creative children finger-tracing of words on cards and allocation of cards to a file is a cumbersome business. Provided that the child looks carefully at the word that has been written and closes his personal dictionary before writing it in his composition, the learning of the word has been initiated. The intention to remember has been retained, if only for the space of time it takes to write the word. There is a theoretical issue here in that immediate checking has not been catered for. There is a calculated risk that a word may have been written incorrectly, especially if the span of the word is longer than about six letters. The practice of taking the personal dictionary and checking the words asked for and acquired during the past lesson would partly remedy this. In any case the first learning should be consolidated in the formal learning of the child's own needed and asked-for words, at a later time. Thus, this learning is subsidiary to, and an integral part of, the child's creative writing.

It is, of course, essential that the word should be acquired with no delay so that the sentence continues to flow without interruption. It is important to establish habits, for example, of the child presenting the 'dictionary' open at the correct page, so that the teacher can write the word quickly and the child look at it and *learn* the look of it as he returns to his desk. In a class-room climate where creative writing is encouraged and cherished, the teacher's quick response avoids delay, and in the writer's experience, there has never been known what is so inimical to lively learning and expression, a queue! To avoid having to ask for all words, certain common words can, of course, be made available in word-lists, and common nouns can be acquired from a picture dictionary. Obviously i.t.a. taught children can, in the early stages, write without any need to ask for words, since their writing is unexceptionally phonic. The habit they acquire of writing at length is indeed a good habit of expression to acquire. It is at a later stage, after transfer to t.o. that the techniques described above would need to be exercised.

Active self-testing is perhaps the most effective method of learning material such as spelling, and for the consolidation of this learning the teacher in the Infant or early Junior School classes, and later the children themselves, can write the words asked for in a note-book with folded pages to provide space where the child can test and re-test himself without copying, since the word is hidden before the child writes the word. This avoids the need for the formulation of elaborate rules, as repeated examples of words within the child's vocabulary provide the repetition of examples necessary. Often it is only when a rule is pointed out to a habitually good speller that doubts begin to occur. This avoids the need for a test-study procedure, as the children will only be learning the words they do not know, yet need to know, and recognize that they need to know, and are therefore motivated to learn. This avoids, too, the use of carefully graded word lists suited to a certain age, as the words are in the children's own idiom. Some children, who are less able linguistically, will ask for less sophisticated words than children who are verbally adventurous, but they will be learning to write the words *they* need. And spelling is an essential skill only in so far as we want to write. A good speller who never puts pen to paper is like a good linguist who never speaks or reads the language he knows.

Some spelling errors will occur, however. Children will 'think they know' a word. They will, engrossed in the development of their story, flow on without asking, and memory images can deceive. It is so easy in reading creative writing for the teacher to notice the *errors*, not the strength and vividness of composition, and easier still when wielding the red pencil. To avoid too much attention to the errors, and to co-operate with the child in producing a well-presented and correct piece of writing, the child could write his stories and diary in pencil, so that the teacher can rub out the spelling errors, preferably in the child's presence. He himself should fill in the words which the teacher has written correctly in his dictionary. What is more, the intention to spell a word correctly may well transfer some habit of care and satisfaction in the production of an orderly and well-presented piece of writing. This is an integrated approach that demands rigours of learning and execution, though not at the expense of creative writing. For, as Hildreth (1956, 34) writes, 'Teachers should not think of incidental learning and integrated teaching as excluding systematic, well-organized drill. Rather from the child's attempts to write will come the need for systematic word study.'

Throughout this approach to the teaching of spelling, emphasis has been laid on looking, on noticing the sequences of letters, on motivation to perceive and retain the percept in the interests of free spontaneous creative writing, in fact on the exploitation of sight which is our preferred sense.

Environmental reinforcement of such learning

Such sensory preference is indeed exploited on every hand, and reinforced wherever we turn. In 1966 we are bombarded with visual verbal stimuli. A generation ago few neon signs excited Piccadilly, and advertisements were sober and informative. The village inn, once distinguished only by the life-size wooden fox chased along the wall by life-size hounds, is now clearly labelled 'Fox and Hounds' and the brewer's name. Towns and villages are named with unmistakable clarity as one approaches them in cars that no longer bear merely the cryptic flying A, or the leaping panther. Now they are clearly named, Austin Cambridge, Jaguar Mark IV, and even described with the single terse qualification, overdrive. But it is in advertising that we are most bombarded. Publicity agents no longer present vague muddled descriptive advertising, but stark names and startling slogans, and these appear most arrestingly and repetitively in commercial television. The reading level of T.V. advertising is about 7 to 8 years; the lightning episodes are often as appealing and dramatic to the 5 to 7 year old as the domestic and familiar episodes they are invited to listen to or watch with mother. Indeed young children have been observed to stop playing and look up with eager interest when advertisements appear. But the stimulus to learning is in the fact that these short, neat, simple phrases are not only repeated aurally but thrown simultaneously on to the screen. We are advised six times to 'Bridge that gap'. We are repeatedly informed 'Your cat will stay younger, live longer.' The word 'acid' is projected as a flash-card on to the screen for three seconds at a time. All the technical skill and artifices of films, cartoons and television are tapped to provide intensity, change, size, repetition in the stimuli and to appeal to our basic needs of ascendancy, hunger, sex, maternal feeling, acquisitiveness. The words and names are not only presented in an inviting situation but also fulfil the demands made by the laws of learning, repetition, spaced learning, presentation in two sensory modalities simultaneously. Finally, television being so highly compulsive, children are well motivated to watch, and they focus, particularly in a poorly lighted room, directly on to the screen. Conditions are perfect for indirect reinforcement of word structure in the case of normally learning children.

Exploitation of modern visual media in the cause of backward spellers

Children who have failed to learn to spell are likely to be children who have never succumbed to verbal stimuli visually. For such children this incidental tool of teaching, this fire-side visual aid can be deliberately exploited, and in the home, anxious parents of backward children can usefully help in remedial teaching. The technique is the same as with the personal dictionary described above. The word must be perceived and retained. Again active self-testing must occur. The word or the phrase must be written from memory, without looking up in the middle, and checked when the word or phrase is repeated on the screen. Parents will frequently co-operate by checking. It is sometimes objected that trade names are unusual, and even incorrect. In fact very few of the 'Kleen-e-ze' variety appear in television advertising, and it is the habit of looking and noting that is important, not the learning to spell of a particular trade-name. This is a technique preparatory to, and essential in the 'caught not taught' art, that is, in the cause of 'incidental learning'. If the incorrect word *is* learned, this will be in conjunction with, and only apply to the product, and not the familiar word, which will have to be taught and pigeon-holed separately. What, anyway, are product names if not nonsense in our own language, since they follow the rules and precedents of our own language?

The problem of homophones

There is still the problem of homophones. Homophones are words that sound the same but look different. As Vallins (1965, 144) says 'they are a natural and necessary by-product of a spelling that preserves in its symbols the etymological origin of words'. An example is the word 'tied' and 'tide'. Now in Scotland these two words neither look the same nor sound the same. 'Tied' to the Scottish sounds quite differently from 'tide' and Scottish children do not make as many homophone errors as English children. For them 'fur' and 'fir' sound quite different, and if a Scottish child is taught phonics well, as many of them are, the problem does not arise. But English children, and particularly those who have failed to learn to spell, and need remedial teaching, have to be taught a method of differentiating homophones, and selecting which of two spellings to choose.

It would seem sensible to teach one of the pair instead of teaching the two together and risking further confusion. Harder (1937) in research on the 'separate' and 'together' method of teaching homophones showed that nine year old children remembered the spellings of homophones best when they had been learned together, whether they were tested immediately or after some delay. Twelve-year-old children however, remembered together learnt homophones best when they were tested immediately. But if there was a delay before testing (and this is like the real-life spelling situation when permanent recall is needed) the homophones were best retained when learned separately.

A method of dealing with such words that sound the same but look different, is to teach one of this pair in relation to other similarly constructed words that have meaningful association.

The problem of phonemic alternatives

It was shown in Chapter 1 that the real problem is not only with phonemically irregular words, but with words that are regular but have quite reasonable phonic alternatives. Faced with the task of writing a word like 'fruit' a child might well select the phoneme 'oo' and write 'froot'. Some words lend themselves to this kind of confusion more than others and need some kind of association to spark off the correct phoneme. Some familiar word must act as a cue to evoke such an association. For example most children have seen the word 'penguin' if only on the label of a biscuit. The word penguin, looked at attentively, is the clue. The sentence 'The penguin spilt fruit juice down his black suit and ruined it', ridiculous as it is, forms an association between the clue 'penguin' and the similarly spelt words, 'fruit', 'juice', 'suit', and 'ruined'. The child needing to write the word 'fruit' or 'suit' or even 'suitable', and insecure about its spelling will refer to the category of spelling pattern embraced in this little story.

It is this sort of association that can be evoked with older children or adults. They must be helped to connect words that have the same visual pattern, that look the same, even though they sound differently. Stories or rhymes containing a number of words that look alike however they sound are presented so that the association is in the story.

'Please *sir* can I *stir* the coffee?
Can I *sir*, I've such a *thirst*?
Look your *skirt* and *shirt* are dirty
Go and wash them *first*.'

'Won't *disturb* the *nurse*'. The *burglar*
Turned the lock and *burst* it open,
Took the *furs*, her *purse* and *hurled* them
Through the *curtains*. '*Curse*' she's woken.
Surly now, *he murmured*, softly
'No *surprise*, no *hurt*, no *murder*.
If *pursued*, I'll *burst* the *church*.
And *burn* them in the *furnace* there.'
'What's your *purpose*?' called the *nurse*,
'*Return* my *furs* and *purse*, and please
On *Thursday purchase* and *refurnish*
Curtains, locks for me, and keys.'

Come the end of winter *terms*,
Water flows, the *river* rises,
Over moss and *ferns*. We long for
Summer and the end of *germs*.

The child needing to spell the word 'thirst' or 'disturb' will then connect with one particular episode.

To make the fullest use of such associations, the child should learn the *italicized* words, writing them out (not blindly copying but remembering each word as a whole before he writes it), and writing the whole story or verse from dictation, in other words he should be using associative clues, attending to visual structure, reinforcing visual imagery and actively self-testing as he learns. In addition the remedial teacher will note the kinds of words the child or student fails in, and will build on former learning. For example, if a student makes repeated mistakes with words like 'conscious' or 'conscience' these can be built upon the word 'science'.

The intention is that ultimately the older child or student will use unhesitatingly the probable sequence of letters in any word. Such sequences will become so familiar that, faced eventually with the need to spell new and unfamiliar words, the correct sequence flows.

5

The assessment of spelling: how spelling is tested

If we want to know how good a child is at spelling there are several ways of finding out. We can look at his written work and see how many mistakes he makes, but the judgement we make is subjective. We are at most comparing his spelling with that of other children in his class who most probably are writing on other topics and using words of a different level of difficulty. So it is necessary to standardize what he and the other children are writing, and to do this eliminates for each child not only his choice of the word he is to spell, but the use of that word in the child's own phrase and idiom. It also eliminates the mental set to 'get it down' in the context of the story he is writing, and most important of all, his own personal mental process from the idea to the imaged, perhaps articulated, written word.

The testing approach commonly assumed to approximate most nearly to this process is dictation of the kind of words the children are most likely to need but may mis-spell. But the teacher's pronunciation may be strange, and she may enunciate the words indistinctly, so it is necessary to put the words in the framework of a sentence.

Even so the sentence has not the immediacy or the turn of the child's own phrase. The kind of sentences we use to incorporate e.g. the word 'breathe' (Schonell S.2. spelling norm 12+). 'We *breathe* the fresh air,' has not the urgency that it has in five-year-old Fiona's sentence in her diary, 'I am a dragon. I breathe fire.' A sentence we may use to embed the word 'ground'. (Schonell S.1. spelling norm 8+) 'let us sit on the *ground*', has not the overtones of the nine-year-old's writing, 'The *ground* was slimy and moist and as I slivered down I found myself in a lovely garden where the snap dragons were dragons and flowers came to life,' though the word 'breathe' or 'ground' is equally clearly enunciated and the concept understood.

Dictation type tests (recall)

Dictation type tests are however the kind most used in schools. Burt's 'Graded Spelling Vocabulary Test' (1921) and Schonell's Graded Spelling Test S.1. and S.2. (1932) consisting of 10 words for each year, are such. In Burt's test the words are dictated separately, but not incorporated in sentences. This makes the test quicker to administer, but the norms are now very old. The words in Schonell's tests are 'first dictated, next embedded in an explanatory sentence and then dictated again'.

A similar but much more recently standardized test in which the words have to be incorporated in sentences is Daniel's and Diack's Graded Spelling Test (1958). This only gives norms up to 12·3 years, so does not cover the upper attainment levels even of the primary school. It is, however, very easy to mark and use diagnostically, since it separates in four lists, words of different levels of use and spelling difficulty. All these tests can be given as group tests, but with a wide range of ability it may be necessary to administer the whole test, many words being too easy for the best spellers, many being too difficult for the poorest spellers.

An alternative to dictating the words is to evoke the words by means of pictures and stories which are 'read together' (Lambert's *Seven Plus Assessment*, 1951). The norms here are for children from 7 to 8. Fleming's *Kelvin Measurement of Spelling Ability* (1933) is a dictation test in which the sentence dictated appears on the test-form with a blank for the child to write in the missing but dictated word. The norms are from 7 to 12 years.

We would expect that the dictation kind of test would be most valid. Yet a dictation test is a test of recall and we all know that it is harder to recall a word than to recognize it. Would recognition tests serve the same purpose?

Multiple choice tests (recognition)

There are several types of recognition tests of spelling, all published ones being American, in which

- (a) incorrectly spelt words are to be identified. 'Underline the words spelt wrongly.'
- (b) correctly spelt words are to be identified. 'Underline the words spelt correctly.'
- (c) given the beginning and end of a word, the troublesome middle to be written in. 'Complete the word.'
- (d) given a meaningful sentence containing an incorrectly spelt word to be corrected. 'Find and underline the word spelt wrongly. Then write it.'

Validity of the two types of test

Surprisingly Cook (1932) suggested that a multiple choice test of this kind was the most valid test of spelling in free writing, since in neither does the child know which words need special care. This would seem an unlikely criterion

of validity. Indeed there would seem to be a major difference between the two situations in their different perceptual approach. In free writing the child is sub-vocally
articulating and perhaps using auditory imagery and discrimination.

In the error recognition type of test he is at first visually
scanning words, then visually discriminating and finally
calling on visual memory images as a check.

Nisbet (1939) found that these recognition tests measured
much the same ability as recall (dictation) tests. He also
showed that tests using wrongly spelt words, and, even
more, skeleton words, were superior to multiple choice
tests. Little attention was paid to this problem until in
the light of a Swedish investigation by Wallin (1962, quoted
by Ahlstrom, 1964) it was suggested that the auditory demands made on the child helped in a dictation type of test
(recall) more than in a multiple choice type of test (recognition). To find whether recognition and recall tests of
spelling do involve the same functions and whether either
kind of test measures the spelling ability needed in free
writing, a Swedish investigation has been initiated
(Ahlstrom, 1964). There were three kinds of spelling activity
to look at, words tested by dictation (mainly auditory cues),
words tested by multiple choice tests (mainly visual cues)
and words spontaneously written (with very little in the
way of external visual and auditory cues). The results show
that there are marked differences between the three kinds
of test, but that dictation tests depend more on auditory
discrimination than multiple choice tests or spontaneous
spelling. Apart from this expected result, something very
interesting emerged. This was that all three types of test
reflected 'knowledge of spelling rules, and this was the best
predictor in all three forms of test'.

Now this 'knowledge of spelling rules' in the Swedish
tests was a predictor derived from the following two tests.

In the first the child saw a meaningless word written down, and selected one of two alternative pronunciations he heard spoken. In the second test the child's task was to predict not pronunciation but spelling. He heard a meaningless word and had to write the appropriate symbol of one of the sounds in the context of the word in which a gap had been left. Ability in this kind of situation would seem to be less a matter of knowing spelling rules than of knowing serial probability, that is of being accustomed to certain sequences of letters occurring. This, as has already been suggested, would seem to be the main plank on which spelling ability depends. (This is a matter not so much of visual discrimination which is so important in reading if 'brain' is not to be read as 'drain', but a matter of visual and motor habits.)

Standardization criteria

In all these tests it is customary, when assessing a child's attainment, to compare his achievement with that of many other children of his own age, and of children slightly younger, and slightly older, giving us an attainment age, e.g. a reading age or a spelling age. This is usually compared with the child's chronological age. Sometimes an achievement quotient is calculated by finding the percentage of one to the other. At one time the achievement age was compared with a hypothetical 'mental age', but this is a practice now rejected for various reasons. It is not far-fetched to envisage comparing the attainment age with a more realistic criterion such as Tanner's suggested skeletal age (1961), if this ever became the accepted yard-stick of physical progress throughout school life.

Testing spelling contrasted with testing reading

At present such an attainment age gives us a comparison

of how a child stands in relation to other children of his own age. This is a useful guide to placement, and to what we expect of children, but it implies that ability in spelling develops year by year, that for example, at 8 most children can spell phonically regular words, such as 'ground' but that at 9 they are beginning to manage irregular words, like 'through' and 'daughter'. This is indeed what happens in attainment tests in reading. As children read better they can manage more words at each age-level, even in the artificial situation of word-reading tests where words are isolated and there is no contribution from context, and no 'mental set' on the part of the child.

There are, in fact, distinctly different levels of reading ability which must have been reached if one is to be equipped to cope with certain levels of reading material. For example, with a reading age of $9\frac{1}{2}$ a child can satisfactorily read much of the *Daily Mirror*, yet not be able to read James Bond. There are also different reading techniques a child must possess in order to deal with different kinds of reading material. Again a completely different approach is needed in skimming through a book, looking for relevant specific items than in following a close argument in a philosophical text. For the one 'faster reading' may indeed be recommended but for the other 'slower reading' may well be the necessary discipline.

Spelling, then, is different from reading in three main ways. First, reading skill is flexible. Considerable variance is possible in performance, depending on the purpose for which one is reading, but in spelling such variance is not acceptable. Spelling does not vary according to the occasion, except in so far as shorthand takes the place of longhand when a secretary receives dictation. Secondly, reading permits successive approximations to the word being read, before commitment, while in spelling, once one has committed oneself on paper, there is no going back. Thirdly, skill in reading is progressive, in the sense that it improves year by year with experience and practice. Spelling on the other hand is much more an all-or-none activity according to the individual's approach, his perceptual habits, his imagery, his attitude, casual or otherwise and most of all, his self-image.

For these reasons, to test spelling in the way one tests reading, by a word-reading test, ten to a year, progressively, is irrational. There is, however, a case for making attainment tests in spelling give way to predictive tests, possibly at the pre-spelling stage, diagnostic tests and classifying tests.

Predictors of good spelling as an all-or-none skill

Instead of asking 'Does this child of eight spell like other children of eight?' we could usefully ask, 'Is this child on the way to becoming a good speller? Are his perceptual habits well-formed? Is he suitably 'set' to learn words as he meets them? In the light of his performances in other fields, where could he be placed on such a grading scale as this:

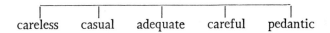

careless   casual   adequate   careful   pedantic

Does he pursue the direct attack that characterises the good speller?' and perhaps the most revealing question of all, 'Does he see himself as a good or poor speller?'

Hartmann (1931), who attributed spelling success to one special form of visual reaction involved in reproducing tachistoscopically exposed but meaningful material, suggested that to use the meaningful perceptual span technique would be an alternative to conventional spelling testing, since it had the advantage of brevity. Certainly this could be a method of screening children who might need to be provided with supplementary perceptual inroads, especially if confirmed by the teachers' assessment of a child's position on the careless—pedantic continuum. In other words a child, who was able to reproduce words exposed very briefly on flash cards, and whose approach in other fields of learning was careful, might be expected to be one of those children who in a 'test-study' learning situation would advance in a spelling programme more quickly than one who found it difficult to reproduce briefly exposed words and whose general attitude was casual. These are predictors of success in spelling, and not tests of how a child stands in relation to children of his own age. They are guides to one approach to the teaching of spelling rather than checks on what has been taught.

Diagnostic tests

Attainment tests tell us where a child stands in relation to children of his own age in specific spelling situations, not necessarily the essential one of spelling correctly in the course of his own free writing. Certain predictors tell us whether children are, or are not, in the way of becoming good spellers. Some children, however, make very low scores in attainment tests. For them there may be little positive prediction of spelling ability. They may be generally casual in attitudes; they may be convinced that they are poor spellers; they may find it very difficult to reproduce words briefly exposed on flash cards, which is fundamental to recognizing and recalling common letter sequences, a skill which is presumably very much allied to the Swedish 'knowledge of spelling rules'. To such children it is usual to present diagnostic tests in order to discover the area of failure. In the light of the foregoing argument, that attitudes and habits contribute a good deal to spelling success, there might seem to be slight justification for diagnostic tests of spelling. In accepting, however, that a child needs diagnostic testing with a view to remedial help in spelling, the teacher implicitly accepts the need for a change in the child's attitude to himself as a poor speller, a change in his attention to details and carefulness in other spheres. She accepts, also, the need for training in immediate memory techniques of visually presented material.

Schonell (1942, 290), was aware of these needs, these 'temperamental attitudes and environmental difficulties', but appreciated that there were individual differences in the children presented for diagnosis of spelling disability. He was very concerned with 'determining for remedial purpose how far the backward speller's visual perception or auditory perception is weak through organic, mental or environmental causes', and constructed three tests for this purpose.

Test S. 4 was to test immediate recall of meaningful three-letter words presented visually on large cards, first three at a time, and increasing by one each time until eight were presented at a time, at the exposure rate of one letter per second. The first list was

> GEM
> BIB
> SUN.

Test S. 5 was to test immediate recall of meaningful three-letter words presented auditorily, first three words at a time, then four and so on. The first list was

> JET
> SAP
> FEN.

Test S. 6. The last was to test immediate recall of nonsense syllables presented visually in the same way as Test S. 4.

The first list was

> JED
> KIB
> VEL.

This was, Schonell suggested, 'an estimate of the pupil's power to handle new linguistic forms'. As these were remote from commonly used letter sequences, their diagnostic value is in pin-pointing a child's immediate memory for material presented visually. To what extent he can perceive, retain and reproduce words he has never seen before is something we should indeed know about any backward speller for whom advice is sought.

Schonell's diagnostic tests S. 4, S. 5, and S. 6 can be administered to a whole class and there are norms available for children between 7 and 13 years. Analysis of results often reflect the child's own individual reading strength pattern. Robert's notes read, 'Tests reveal his superior auditory attack reminiscent of his remedial reading programme when visual attack was poor.' Though he had found phonic analysis unpalatable, this had been a necessary element in his remedial programme, and in order to improve his spelling his newly acquired phonic knowledge had to be exploited and words taught to him in groups according to their sound and phonic pattern. On the other hand, Ian's score was much higher on visual presentation. He had, in spite of a history of speech defect and poor auditory imagery, previously been taught by a strong phonic system. Remedial work in spelling involved training in new habits of looking.

It is possible to expose such emphases in a much simpler way, by, for example, looking diagnostically at the response in a reversed digit test, as presented in a battery intelligence test. To repeat a list of digits in reverse order, the child can either image the digits visually and 'read' them off mentally from right to left, or using auditory imagery, repeat the sequence in correct order mentally and the last digit orally.

For example, presented with 5—9—3—7—8—2 and asked to repeat these backwards he will say '2—8'—then recall auditorily 5—9—3—7 and say '7' recall auditorily 5—9—3 and say '3' and so on.

This is a slower, more hesitant process and recognizable to the tester often without the subject's introspection. It merely reveals a technique of spelling a word out loud, and is not necessarily the technique used in calling up words of which one is unsure: It is perhaps a simpler yet not less valid a means of eliciting a child's method of auditory or visual recall than Schonell's tests, though it does not reveal, as S. 6 does, the ability to reproduce new linguistic forms briefly exposed.

A much more elaborate diagnostic test is the Gates–Russell diagnostic programme (1940), designed to be administered individually and consisting of nine tests to expose the methods of spelling a child uses, what kinds of error he tends to make, and with what success a child is able to learn new words. The test is long, time-consuming, and mainly useful in the remedial centre. The tests have been criticized as selected by *a priori* reasoning without a critical analysis of validity and reliability, but the tests are 'useful as the initial steps in the observation of the difficulties of a poor speller. Some of the tests will reveal certain tendencies and skills, others will need to be supplemented by more adequate testing. Several yield no additional information or bear little relationship to the difficulties present in spelling disability.' (Spache, 1953, 201.)

It is not necessary, for example to test for reversals in spelling. Tordrup (1966), showed that reversals in spelling decreased both absolutely and relatively (compared with other types of error) as children got older, and he saw no reason to ascribe reversals to specific factors such as 'directional confusion'. As Spache (1953) pointed out, reversals are due to immaturity of orientation, not a cause of disability. This is supported in the Swedish research where visual discrimination seemed to have no relation to spelling ability. This, it was suggested, was because visual discrimination is trained during early tuition in reading and because any children markedly handicapped in this ability are withdrawn for special help. As spelling ability usually presupposes a measure of reading ability, and reading ability presupposes visual discrimination, it is reasonable to assume that reversals, being a particular example of visual discrimination, will not constitute a major spelling difficulty and need not be specifically sought out.

Analysis of errors

In the effort to find the most valid testing techniques recognition and recall tests have been studied meticulously (Ahlstrom, 1964). But it is to his own free writing that we look for the most useful pieces of evidence in exploring a poor speller's disability. Though this cannot be standardized, as what he writes is different from what anyone else writes, the pattern of his errors can be examined, and an error profile made. This itself reveals an individual's weakness or strength. Spache (1953, 200) pointed out that 'a minimum of 100 misspelled words is necessary for a reliable sample of error tendencies', but a really poor speller will soon make 100 errors and an analysis from a grid to a profile is diagnostically very revealing when studied with a view to individual remedial teaching. It is a time-consuming procedure however, to collect 100 errors from a child's free writing and analyse these. To short-circuit this, the writer has produced and is standardizing diagnostic dictations, for the three final years of the junior school,

8—9 years, 9—10 years, and 10—11 years. The dictations are short stories of the kind a junior school child might write, but incorporating the most common sources of spelling error. Errors are recorded and profiles made which can be compared with standardized profiles, in order to screen children with glaring spelling faults and perceptual habits that are inimical to their spelling.

Poor spelling confronts the teacher whenever she reads her children's compositions. It is easy for her to test whether children can recall certain words that most children of the same age can recall. It is not easy for her to compare their spelling ability in free writing with one another. In addition, if she is prepared to exercise the kind of diagnostic procedures outlined in this chapter and to give due weight to these in the planning of remedial work, she may well be advised to look at the child clinically, at his attitudes and habits, perceptual and motor, and particularly at his attitude to his own spelling ability. She can build on that, giving plenty of opportunity for practice in immediate memory activities with visually presented material, exercise in auditory discrimination, and above all the confidence derived from his self-image of himself as a good speller.

6

The task of the teacher

In the last chapter it was shown that it is no good having tests which have developed in relation to all kinds of assumptions about spelling that are probably in no way justifiable. If one is going to have spelling tests at all, these must relate in some significant way to the determinants of good spelling, and also to defensible methods of the teaching of spelling. It has been argued that the determinants of good spelling may be physiological and psychological. It is more likely that they are educational, deriving from habits acquired in the teaching of reading and spelling skills. This involves the third determinant, the motivational, in the sense that the attitude to the skill exerts a very great influence on success in it. So responsibility for good spelling seems largely to lie in the school. What can the teacher do to help children in this complex and often elusive skill?

Factors revealed by research

Considerable research has been conducted with a view to directing the teacher's approach to specific details of the spelling programme as well as to the more generalized approaches outlined in Chapter 4. The most recent and the most sophisticated piece of research is that already mentioned in connection with the testing of spelling conducted in 1964 and still being followed up in Sweden. In this investigation into the structure of spelling ability, analysis revealed a number of factors involved in spelling. Five main factors were revealed, and these are of immense importance in considering the task of the teacher, since all factors suggest avenues or confirm practices pursued by teachers empirically.

(i) *The verbal factor of reading.* The first factor was shown to be a high verbal factor. This involved language training, for example familiarity with words, their structure and their use. This was the verbal factor Townsend (1947) spotted when she showed the higher correlation between spelling and vocabulary than between spelling and reading comprehension or spelling and tests of academic aptitude, and it is to be expected that word enthusiasts are able to spell well, whether their enthusiasm stems from etymology, trained eloquence or cross-word puzzles. The Swedish analysis showed skill in reading and spelling to be related to each other, but some aspects of reading to be more closely related to spelling than others, particularly reading aloud. 'Reading aloud seems to be associated with skill in spelling, since in principle at least it is possible to read and spell words correctly without having any idea of their meaning.' (Ahlstrom, 1965, 37). Reading aloud entails the auditory analysis which is essential to the spelling of words that are phonemically regular. It also associates the look of the word with the articulated and heard sound of the word. Articulation itself is helped and hence spelling, since children with a very poor spoken language tend to be bad spellers.

(ii) *Knowledge of sequential probability.* An auditory discrimination factor emerged next, involving prediction of pronunciation from a written nonsense word and prediction of spelling from a spoken nonsense word. This is what the Swedes term 'knowledge of spelling rules' and is, as has been argued earlier, very akin to what we would call knowledge of probable letter sequence through precedents. It will be remembered that Wallach (1963, 61) demonstrated that good spellers showed much more transfer of training from familiar to unfamiliar or nonsense words than poor spellers and this, he says, suggests some new implications regarding what one should attempt to teach in order to improve a child's spelling. 'Whereas teaching procedures based on phonetic training have been in use for some time there has been little attempt yet to base training procedures on transfer involving the sequential probability structure of letters'. To effect such transfer, there must occur day by day verbal experiences of every possible variant of spelling pattern in the language. Now Fries (1962, 171-184) enumerates and describes these spelling patterns:

(a) one-syllable words with the general shape of consonant-vowel-consonant, e.g. mad.
(b) spelling-patterns using the final 'e' to differentiate them from e.g. made.
(These two cover a large part of the active practices of English.)
(c) a number of important spelling-patterns of much more limited application, involving the varied doubled vowels.

These three major sets of spelling pattern form the basis of the modern English spelling we have to learn. We must, he points out, for example, as writers learn to spell the unstressed syllables of each word, e.g. sound patterns with the same vowel phoneme in the final syllable, sofa, orphan, silken, sojourn, dragon, handsome, etc. These are all possibilities that children must be aware *can* occur, before they can learn when they *should* occur.

Jensen (1962) showed that spelling errors occur more often in medial than in the beginning or ending of words, and it is the middle phonemes of words that have quite reasonable alternatives that are the cause of so much difficulty in learning to spell. First the possibilities must be learned. Children must get used to reasonable letter sequences. This is where procedures of the kind suggested in Chapter 4 using modern visual media such as television advertising, are justified. Children are learning the nonsense of their own language, and it is primarily in an informal manner such as this that such learning occurs. This is where incidental learning is really justified, where children usefully catch the flavour and vagaries of their own language structure. It might be thought that children who are taught to read by i.t.a. are being deprived of this opportunity to learn the nonsense of their own language. This would indeed be the case if they did not constantly and inevitably receive the impact of such verbal stimuli in traditional orthography through advertisements, names and signs. Without this impact they would be immune from those very irregularities and idiosyncrasies the initial teaching alphabet is, by definition, avoiding. Before spelling learning can be really effective, children must be aware of the probable structures of words in their language. There are, of course, less informal ways in which such awareness is brought about. The infant teacher writes on the child's picture captions that the child dictates. He watches and is satisfied with his own verbalization. The mother reads to her child, and the child follows as she reads. The father, as he drives along, reads the names of towns, villages and streets and the children articulate the names and words as they see them. The teacher lets the children give out named books and boxes, so that the children become familiar with

Christian names that are characteristic of the spelling patterns of their own language structure. Children, too, are constantly requesting words to be put in their finger-tracing file or their personal dictionary, and here they are learning the possibilities of spelling pattern.

More systematic observation of word-structure is important however. Freyberg (1964) showed that poor spellers fared better if they were taught from spelling lists compiled by the teacher than from individual lists, and he advocates teacher-provided lists for poorer spellers and perhaps for younger children. What sort of lists should the teacher provide? To show that unusual sequences have other examples and precedents she should provide lists of words that look and sound the same. These will be short lists of words like door, floor; or word, world; or worse, worst, worry; or weigh, weight, eight, freight (since the new designation on goods vehicles) and these are presented as :

(*a*) reading lists.
(*b*) look, cover up and write lists.

Children can work individually or in pairs. Sets of such cards, the size of railway tickets, are inevitably expendable, since children can be given the cards to carry home in their pockets to look at from time to time.

And as all the possible sequences are being learned and children are becoming used to reasonable letter sequences, the procedure for transfer mentioned by Wallach is further consolidated by day to day drills involving finger-tracing techniques, and techniques of looking with intent to recall and writing from memory, of every possible variant of spelling pattern in the language when words are needed for free writing.

(iii) *Immediate memory for visual material.* Next emerged

a factor representing immediate memory for visual material. Now this is something which it has been found possible to train. It will be remembered that Hartmann (1931) showed that good spellers were distinguished by their immediate memory span for meaningful visual stimuli, and Gilbert and Gilbert (1942) in a Flash card method demonstrated the possibility of decreasing perceptual time while increasing proficiency in both immediate and delayed recall. Mason (1961) found that nonsense syllables proved as effective as real words for developing the visual discrimination necessary to improve spelling, and a Secondary teacher, Garrity (1963) working with Secondary children advocated 'concentration sessions', presenting random letters auditorily and visually, increasing the span each time. If instead of random letters, nonsense approximations to English were aimed at, this could well fulfil two needs. It could increase the span of apprehension and exercise serial probability at the same time.

It will be recalled too that Radaker (1963) showed that training in imagery improved spelling performance significantly over long periods of time. Radaker's methods of testing the value of imagery practice was with nonsense words. The children, aged 8½ to 10½ years, were told to close their eyes and try to arouse an image of the word in large, glossy black letters on a white background. It was suggested that the word should be visualized as though it were projected on a large outdoor theatre screen. They were to try and stabilize the image and retain it as long as possible, with a maximum objective of one minute for each word. If images proved unstable they should mentally visualize the words in large metallic letters with holes punched in the top and bottom to accommodate pretend nails to which unstable letters could be securely 'nailed'. Retention involved pretend paste applied to the letter backs to 'glue' them into place. Pretend floodlight was invoked and so on. The habit of such imagery practice in the learning of 'asked for' words and words in reputable spelling lists would be a valuable adjunct to the training in immediate memory span. These are the kind of training drills that are practicable in the classroom.

(iv) *The intellectual factor*. The fourth factor is an intellectual factor of an inductive nature. Now such a factor cannot be identified with 'intelligence' as measured by standard intelligence tests. Correlations between spelling and intelligence, as summarized by Russell (1937) from previous research are positive, though not as big as between intelligence and reading. Nevertheless low mental ability, he suggested, may affect spelling ability within certain restricted limits. Let us look at this 'intellectual factor of an inductive nature' more broadly. It is, in the light of previous discussion, obvious that to be aware of the rationale of English spelling takes a child a long way towards being able to spell. It will be remembered that children taught to read in a rule-following manner by a pure phonic method not only continue to spell in a reasonable manner, making when uncertain, reasonable phonic alternatives rather than haphazard shots at a word, but also look on written language as something fairly reasonable. Is it far fetched to suggest that such an outlook is conducive to working inductively, and that the intellectual factor of an inductive nature drawn out in factor analysis by the Swedes, can be more readily tapped by individuals who look on written language as a reasonable and manageable medium?

(v) *Interest in reading*. Finally there is an 'interest in reading factor' deriving from attitude to books and book borrowing habits. In this factor is loaded word-identification which, it is to be expected, is a characteristic of the fast and avid reader.

Techniques of study

One factor that has repeatedly appeared in research writings as conducive to good spelling ability, involves good techniques of study. In two investigations Gilbert and Gilbert (1942) showed that 'limiting study time may work to the advantage of the learner'. In investigation into the effects of teaching spelling through insistence on speed and accuracy of visual perception, they concluded that the most important task for the teacher was the proper marshalling of effort. Good techniques of study should involve finding the optimum study rate of pupils. Time spent on visual examination of the word should be limited, since they found that judicious training could effect an increase in rate and efficiency, and improve perceptual habits. They were quite clear that the practice of assigning words to be studied for an unlimited period was unprofitable and undesirable. Spelling should be taught, definite instructions being given as to how to learn, and should proceed as quickly as possible. In a study of eye-movements, Gilbert described one of the most efficient twelve-year-old spellers who, in the pre-test wrote 'definitely' as 'definitly'. In the subsequent learning of its spelling, however, her eye-movement record showed that she paid very little attention to the 'e' she had previously omitted. Another twelve year old, in learning to spell the word 'questionnaire', spent most of the learning period on the study of the word 'question' which she had spelled correctly in the pre-test. In spite of 'knowing' the word, she studied it! It is as long ago as 1919 that Horn advised us to test words before teaching. It was to avoid this kind of wasted time and effort in unnecessary learning that test-study rather than study-test methods were evolved (Fitzgerald, 1953). Freyberg (1960) advocates a positive approach to the teaching of spelling, a systematic approach demanding set word-study periods and autonomy of learning.

Before summarizing the task of the teacher in establishing the best conditions under which children will learn to spell competently, let us look back half a century to Horn (1919) and Gill (1912) who put a case for systematic instruction in spelling. 'There is no short cut to spelling', Horn said, and his five rules for teaching spelling are worth keeping in mind.

Rules

1. Test all words before teaching.
2. Let each child work only on the words difficult for him and provide him with a definite method of learning them.
3. Provide for rigorous reviews.
4. Show the pupil his progress daily, weekly, monthly and yearly.
5. Keep up his interest.

Much research, however, has been done on spelling since those days and it is now possible to expand this advice. It can now be said, in the light of this research, that the task of the teacher in the interest of good spelling ability is to provide for the following:

1. Familiarity with words, their structure and their use, as an essential pre-requisite to learning to spell. (Ahlstrom, 1964)
2. The practice of reading aloud which seems to be associated with skill in spelling. (Ahlstrom, 1964)
3. Training procedures in which poor spellers are presented with nonsense words of varying degrees of approximation to English, and taught to discriminate those that are most like English. (Wallach, 1963)
4. Careful teacher-prepared lists, since poor spellers fare better when taught from spelling lists compiled by the teacher than from individual lists. (Freyberg, 1964)

5. Multi-sensory approaches involving finger-tracing to help children in learning to spell new words. (Fernald, 1943)

6. Training procedures to improve immediate memory span for meaningful visual material, since this is an ability possessed by good spellers. (Hartmann, 1931)

7. Training procedures to decrease perceptual time in learning, concurrently with increased proficiency in immediate and delayed recall, by using graded flash cards (Gilbert and Gilbert, 1942), and as successfully with nonsense syllables as with real words. (Mason, 1961)

8. Training in imagery which improves spelling performance significantly. (Radaker, 1963)

9. Encouragement of rule-following approaches to the teaching of reading, which lead to a more rational approach to spelling. (Peters, 1967)

10. A healthy attitude to books and interest in reading, which is undoubtedly an advantage to spelling. (Ahlstrom, 1964)

11. Finding the optimum study rate of children in learning to spell. (Gilbert and Gilbert, 1942)

12. Limiting study time which may well work to the advantage of the learner. (Gilbert and Gilbert, 1942)

To conclude, Richmond (1960), confirms Horn (1954) in saying that adequate research is available for improving spelling instruction. Marksheffel (1964, 182) adds, 'But the problem of *how* to get teachers to apply the findings of research to their class-room practices remains.' The resurgence of interest in spelling through the work of people like Freyberg and Arvidson, who advocate a positive and systematic approach to spelling, and such people as Fries in Linguistics, and Bruner and Wallach in coding systems, should solve the problem of how to get all these findings applied in the classroom. The application of research findings will occur when the attitude of teachers to spelling is more positive, so that the attitude of the children themselves to spelling is such that they acquire, from the very beginning, a positive self-image about themselves as good spellers.

Bibliography

ABERCROMBIE, M. L. J. (1964) *Perceptual and Visuo-motor Disorders in Cerebral Palsy*, Heinemann.

AHLSTROM, K. G. (1964) *Studies of Spelling*, Institute of Education, Uppsala University.

ANDREWS, R. (1964) Research Study No. 9, University of Queensland Papers, Faculty of Education, i, No. 4.

ARVIDSON, G. L. (1963) *Learning to Spell*, Wheaton.

AYRES, L. P. (1913) *The Spelling Vocabularies of Personal and Business Letters*, Russell Sage Foundation, New York.

BERNARD, A. M. (1961) 'An Experimental Study in Spelling', *Supplement to Scottish Educational Journal*, V. (June 1931) described in *Studies in Spelling*. University of London Press, 1961.

BIXLER, H. (1940) *The Standard Elementary Spelling Scale*, Turner E. Smith & Co., Atlanta.

BREED, F. S. (1925) 'What Words Should Children Be Taught to Spell?' *Elementary School Journal*, xxvi, (1925) 118-131, 202-214, 292-306.

BRUNER, J. S. and HARCOURT, R.A.F. (1953) *Going Beyond the Information Given*, Unpublished manuscript (1953).

BURT, C. (1962) *Mental and Scholastic Tests*, 4th edition, Staples.

COOK, W. A. and O'SHEA, M. V. (1914) *The Child and His Spelling*, Bobbs-Merrell, Indianapolis.

COOK, W. W. (1932) *The Measurement of General Spelling Ability Involving Controlled Comparison Between Techniques*, University of Iowa Studies in Education, vi.

CORNMAN, O. P. (1902) *Spelling in the Elementary School*, Ginn, Boston.

DANIELS, J. G. and DIACK, H. (1958) *The Standard Reading Tests*, Chatto and Windus.

BIBLIOGRAPHY

DIACK, H. (1960) *Reading and the Psychology of Perception,* Peter Skinner Publishing Ltd.

DOUGLAS, J. W. B. (1964) *The Home and the School,* MacGibbon and Kee.

EDUCATION, BOARD OF (1923) 'Mental and Scholastic Tests Among Retarded Children', *Board of Education Pamphlet,* 44, by H. Gordon.

EDWARDS, R. P. A. and GIBBON, V. (1964) *Words Your Children Use,* Burke, London.

ELDRIDGE, R. C. (1911) *Six Thousand Common English Words,* The Clement Press, Buffalo.

FENDRICK, P. (1935) *Visual Characteristics of Poor Readers,* Contributions to Education, No. 656, New York Bureau of Publications.

FERNALD, G. M. (1943) *Remedial Techniques in Basic School Subjects,* McGraw-Hill, New York.

FITZGERALD, J. A. (1953) 'The Teaching of Spelling', *Elementary English,* xxx (1953) 79-85.

FLEMING, C. M. (1933) *Kelvin Measurement of Spelling Ability,* Robert Gibson and Sons, Glasgow.

FORAN, T. G. (1934) *The Psychology and Teaching of Spelling,* Catholic Education Press, Washington D.C.

FREYBERG, P. S. (1960) *Teaching Spelling to Juniors,* Macmillan.

FREYBERG, P. S. (1964) 'A Comparison of Two Approaches to the Teaching of Spelling', *British Journal of Educational Psychology,* xxxiv (1964) 178-186.

FRIES, C. C. (1962) *Linguistics and Reading,* Holt, Rinehart and Winston.

FULTON, M. J. (1914) 'An Experiment in Teaching Spelling', *Pedagogical Seminary,* xxi (1914) 287-9.

GARRITY, J. (1963) Communication arising from *Teachers' Investigation into Spelling,* Unpublished report, 1963.

GATES, A. I. (1931) 'An experimental comparison in the Study-test and the Test-study Methods in Spelling', *Journal of Educational Psychology,* xxii, (1931), 1-19.

GATES, A. I. (1937) *Spelling Difficulties in 3876 Words,* New York Bureau of Publications Teachers' College, Columbia University.

GATES, A. I. and CHASE, E. H. (1926) 'Methods and theories of learning to spell tested by studies of deaf children', *Journal of Educational Psychology,* xvii (1926), 289-300.

GATES, A. I. and RUSSELL, D. H. (1940) *Diagnostic and Remedial Spelling Manual,* New York Bureau of Publications, Teachers' College, Columbia.

GILBERT, L. C. (1935) 'Study of the effect of reading on spelling', *Journal of Educational Research,* (1935) xxviii, 570-576.

GILBERT, L. C. and GILBERT, D. W. (1942) 'Training for speed and accuracy of visual perception in learning to spell'. *California University Publications in Education,* VII, No. 5 (1942), 351-426.

GILL, E. J. (1912) 'The Teaching of Spelling', *Journal of Experimental Pedagogy*, i (1912), 310.

GREENE, H. A. (1954) *The New Iowa Spelling Scale*, State University of Iowa, Bureau of Educational Research and Service.

GROFF, P. J. (1961) 'The New Iowa Spelling Scale: How Phonetic is it?', *Elementary School Journal*, lxii (1961), 46-49.

HANNA, P. R. and MOORE, J. T. (1953) 'Spelling from Spoken Word to Written Symbol', *Elementary School Journal*, liii (1953), 329-37.

HARDER, K. C. (1937) 'The Relative Efficiency of the Separate and Together Methods of Teaching Homonyms', *Juronal of Experimental Education*, vi (1937) 7-23.

HARTMANN, G. W. (1931) 'The Relative Influence of Visual and Auditory Factors in Spelling Ability', *Journal of Educational Psychology*, xxii, 9, (1931), 691-699.

HIGLEY, B. R. and B. M. (1936) 'An Effective Method of Learning to Spell', *Educational Research Bulletin*, xv, No. 9. Columbus-Ohio State University.

HILDERBRANDT, E. (1923) 'The Psychological Analysis of Spelling', *Pedagogical Seminary*, xxx, (1923), 371-381.

HILDRETH, G. H. (1953) 'Inter-Grade Comparisons of Word Frequencies in Children's Writing', *Journal of Educational Psychology*, xliv, 7, (1953), 429-435.

HILDRETH, G. H. (1956) *Teaching Spelling*, Henry Holt, New York.

HOLMES, J. A. (1959) 'Personality and Spelling Ability', *University of California Publications in Education*, xii, 4 (1959), 213-292.

HORN, E. (1926) 'A Basic Writing Vocabulary: 10,000 Words Most Commonly Used in Writing', *Monographs in Education*, No. 4, University of Iowa.

HORN, E. (1919) 'Principles of Method in Teaching Spelling as Derived from Scientific Investigation', In *National Society for the Study of Education 18th year book Part II*, Bloomington (Ill.), Public School Publishing Co. (1919), 52-77.

HOWES, D. H. and SOLOMON, R. L. (1951) 'Visual duration threshold as a function of word probability'. *Journal of Experimental Psychology*, xli (1951), 401-410.

HUNTER, I. M. L. (1964) *Memory*, Penguin.

JENSEN, A. R. (1962) 'Spelling Errors and the Serial Position Effect', *Journal of Educational Psychology*, liii (1962), 105-109.

JOHNSTON, L. W. (1950) 'One hundred words most often mis-spelled by Children in the Elementary Grades', *Journal of Educational Research*, xliv (1950), 154-55.

KYTE, G. C. (1948) 'When Spelling Has Been Mastered in the Elementary School', *Journal of Educational Research*, xli (1948), 47-53.

LAMBERT, C. M. (1951) *Seven Plus Assessment*, Northumberland Series, University of London Press.

LECKY, P. (1945) *Self-consistency, A Theory of Personality*, Island Press, New York.

BIBLIOGRAPHY

LIVINGSTON, A. A. (1961) 'A Study of Spelling Errors', in *Studies in Spelling*, University of London Press, 1961.

LUKE, E. (1931) *The Teaching of Reading by the Sentence Method*, Methuen.

MCLEOD, M. E. (1961) 'Rules in the Teaching of Spelling', in *Studies in Spelling*, University of London Press, 1961.

MCNALLY, J. and MURRAY, W. (1965) *Key Words to Literacy*, School Master Publishing Company.

MARKSHEFFEL, N. D. (1964) 'Composition, Handwriting and Spelling' in *Review of Educational Research*, xxxiv, 2 (1964), 182-183.

MASON, G. P. (1961) 'Word Discrimination Drills', *Journal of Educational Research*, lv, (1961), 39-40.

MASTERS, H. V. (1927) *A Study of Spelling Errors*, University of Iowa Studies in Education, iv, 4.

MURRAY, E. (1919) 'The Spelling Ability of College Students', *Journal of Educational Psychology*, x, (1919), 357-76.

New Zealand Council for Educational Research (1963) *Alphabetical Spelling List*, Wheaton.

NISBET, S. D. (1939) 'Non-dictated spelling tests', *British Journal of Educational Psychology*, ix, (1939), 29-44.

NISBET, S. D. (1941) 'The Scientific Investigation of Spelling Instruction in Scottish Schools', *British Journal of Educational Psychology*, xi, (1941), 150.

NORRIS, K. E. (1940) *The Three R's and the Adult Worker*, McGill University Press, Montreal.

PETERS, M. L. (1967) 'The Influence of Reading Methods on Spelling', *British Journal of Educational Psychology*, (1967) xxxvii, 47-53.

RADAKAR, L. D. (1963) 'The Effect of Visual Imagery Upon Spelling Performance', *Journal of Educational Research*, lvi, (1963), 370-72.

RICE, J. M. (1897) 'The Futility of the Spelling Grind', *Forum xxiii*, 1897.

RICHMOND, A. E. (1960) 'Children's Spelling Needs and the Implications of Research', *Journal of Experimental Education*, xxix, (1960), 3-21.

RINSLAND, H. D. (1945) *A Basic Writing Vocabulary of Elementary School Children*, Macmillan, New York.

ROSWELL GALLAGHER, J. (1962) 'Word Blindness', in *Word Blindness or Specific Developmental Dyslexia*, Editor, Franklin, A. W., Pitman Medical.

RUSSELL, D. H. (1937) *Characteristics of Good and Poor Spellers*, Contributions to Education No. 727, Bureau of Publications, Columbia Teachers' College.

RUSSELL, D. H. (1955) 'A Second Study of Characteristics of Good and Poor Spellers', *Journal of Educational Psychology*, xlvi, 3, (1955), 129-141.

SCHONELL, F. J. (1934) 'The Relation Between Defective Speech and

Disability in Spelling', *British Journal of Educational Psychology*, iv, 2 (1934), 123-139.

SCHONELL, F. J. (1942) *Backwardness in the Basic Subjects*, Oliver and Boyd.

SCHONELL, F. J. (1932) *Essentials in Teaching and Testing Spelling*, Macmillan.

Scottish Council for Research in Education (1961) *Studies in Spelling*, University of London Press.

Scottish Pupil's Spelling Book (1955) Parts I-V, and *Teacher's Book*, University of London Press Ltd.

SMITH, J. (1961) *Spelling*, Books I to IV, Cassell.

SPACHE, G. (1953) Review of 'Gates-Russell Spelling Diagnosis Test' in the *Fourth Mental Measurements Yearbook*, Gryphon Press, New Jersey, 1953.

SPACHE, G. (1940, *a*) 'A Critical Analysis of Various Methods of Classifying Spelling Errors, I', *Journal of Educational Psychology*, xxxi, 2 (1940, *a*), 11-134.

SPACHE, G. (1940, *b*) 'Validity and reliability of the proposed classification of spelling errors, II', *Journal of Educational Psychology*, xxxi, 3 (1940, *b*), 204-214.

SPACHE, G. (1940, *c*) 'The role of visual defects in spelling and reading disabilities', *American Journal of Orthopsychiatry*, x (1940, *c*), 229-237.

TANNER, J. M. (1961) *Education and Physical Growth*, University of London Press, 1961.

TEMPLIN, M. C. (1954) 'Phonic knowledge and its relation to the spelling and reading achievements of 4th grade pupils', *Journal of Educational Research*, xlvii, (1954), 441-54.

THOMPSON, R. S. (1930) *Effectiveness of Modern Spelling Instruction*, Contributions to Education, No. 436, Teachers' College, New York.

THORNDIKE, E. L. and LORGE, I. (1944) *The Teacher's Word Book*, 3rd edition, Bureau of Publications, Teacher's College, Columbia University.

TORDRUP, S. A. (1966) 'Reversals in Reading and Spelling', *The Slow Learning Child*, xii, 173-183.

TOWNSEND, A. (1947) 'An investigation of certain relationships of spelling with reading and academic aptitude', *Journal of Educational Research*, xl, (1947), 465-71.

VALLINS, G. H. revised by SCRAGG, D. G. (1965) *Spelling*, Deutsch, 1965.

WALLACH, M. A. (1963) 'Perceptual recognition of approximations to English in relation to spelling achievement', *Journal of Educational Psychology*, civ (1963), 57-62.

WALLIN, J. E. W. (1910) 'Has the drill become obsolescent?' *Journal of Educational Psychology*, I (1910), 200-213.

WALTER, W. GREY (1961) *The Living Brain*, Penguin.

87

WASHBURNE, C. (1923) 'A Spelling Curriculum Based on Research', *Elementary School Journal*, xxiii (1923), 751-62.

WATSON, A. (1935) *Experimental Studies in the Psychology and Pedagogy of Spelling*, Contributions to Education, No. 638, Teachers' College, Columbia.

WHEAT, L. B. (1932) 'Four Spelling Rules', *Elementary School Journal*, xxxii, (1932), 697-706.

WOODWORTH, R. S. and SCHLOSBERG, H. (1955) *Experimental Psychology*, Methuen.

Further reading

As most of the literature on spelling is referred to in the text, it is unnecessary to add further notes at this point, except in the case of the following four strongly recommended works:

ARVIDSON, G. L. *Learning to Spell*, Wellington, New Zealand Council for Educational Research, 1960. A Manual for use with the N.Z.C.E.R. Alphabetical Spelling List, but in its own right a most sound and balanced appraisal of spelling needs in school.

HILDRETH, G. H. *Teaching Spelling*, Henry Holt, New York, 1956. An exhaustive guide to basic principles and practices.

Scottish Council for Research in Education, *Studies in Spelling*, University of London Press, 1961. A scholarly report by a panel of workers on their research on spelling.

VALLINS, G. H. revised by SCRAGG, D. G. *Spelling*, Deutsch, 1965. An absorbing analysis of the origins, development and possibilities of English spelling.

Students Library of Education

General Editor   Lionel Elvin

From College to Classroom: The Probationary Year. Derek Hanson and Margaret Herrington. 128 pp.
The Study of Education. J. W. Tibble. 240 pp.

METHOD

Change in Art Education. Dick Field. 132 pp.
Changing Aims in Religious Education. Edwin Cox. 108 pp.
Children and Learning to Read. Elizabeth J. Goodacre. 128 pp.
Discovery Learning in the Primary School. John Foster. 158 pp.
Environmental Studies. D. G. Watts. 128 pp.
*The Future of the Sixth Form.** A. D. C. Peterson. 96 pp.
*Inspecting and the Inspectorate.** John Blackie. 112 pp.
*The Learning of History.** D. G. Watts. 128 pp.
*The Middle School Experiment.** Reese Edwards. 112 pp.
Reading in Primary Schools. Geoffrey R. Roberts. 108 pp.
Spelling: Caught or Taught? Margaret L. Peters. 96 pp.
Students into Teachers: Experiences of Probationers in Schools. Mildred Collins. 112 pp.

HISTORY

*Advisory Councils and Committees in Education.** Maurice Kogan and Tim Packwood. 136 pp.
The American Influence on English Education. W. H. G. Armytage. 128 pp.
The Changing Sixth Form in the Twentieth Century. A. D. Edwards. 115 pp.
*Church, State and Schools in Britain 1800–1970.** James Murphy. 192 pp.
*English Education and the Radicals 1780–1850.** Harold Silver. 148 pp.
*English Primary Education and the Progressives 1914–1939.** R. J. W. Selleck. 206 pp.
The Evolution of the Comprehensive School 1926–1972. David Rubinstein and Brian Simon. 148 pp.
The Evolution of the Nursery-Infant School. Nanette Whitbread. 160 pp.

The Foundations of Twentieth-Century Education. E. Eaglesham. 128 pp.

The French Influence on English Education. W. H. G. Armytage. 128 pp.

*The German Influence on English Education. W. H. G. Armytage. 142 pp.

Mediaeval Education and the Reformation. J. Lawson. 128 pp.

Recent Education from Local Sources. Malcolm Seaborne. 128 pp.

*The Russian Influence on English Education. W. H. G. Armytage. 138 pp.

Secondary School Reorganization in England and Wales. Alun Griffiths. 128 pp.

Social Change and the Schools: 1918–1944. Gerald Bernbaum. 128 pp.

The Social Origins of English Education. Joan Simon. 132 pp.

PHILOSOPHY

Education and the Concept of Mental Health. John Wilson. 99 pp.

Indoctrination and Education. I. A. Snook. 128 pp.

Interest and Discipline in Education. P. S. Wilson. 142 pp.

The Logic of Education. P. H. Hirst and R. S. Peters. 196 pp.

Philosophy and the Teacher. Edited by D. I. Lloyd. 180 pp.

The Philosophy of Primary Education. R. F. Dearden. 208 pp.

Plato and Education. Robin Barrow. 96 pp.

Problems in Primary Education. R. F. Dearden. 160 pp.

PSYCHOLOGY

Creativity and Education. Hugh Lytton. 144 pp.

Group Study for Teachers. Elizabeth Richardson. 144 pp.

Human Learning: A Developmental Analysis. H. S. N. McFarland. 136 pp.

An Introduction to Educational Measurement. D. Pidgeon and A. Yates. 122 pp.

Modern Educational Psychology: An Historical Introduction. E. G. S. Evans. 118 pp.

An Outline of Piaget's Developmental Psychology. Ruth M. Beard. 144 pp.

Personality, Learning and Teaching. George D. Handley. 126 pp.

*Teacher Expectations and Pupil Learning. Roy Nash. 128 pp.

Teacher and Pupil: Some Socio-Psychological Aspects. Philip Gammage. 128 pp.

Troublesome Children in Class. Irene E. Caspari. 160 pp.

SOCIOLOGY

Basic Readings in the Sociology of Education. D. F. Swift. 368 pp.
Class, Culture and the Curriculum. Denis Lawton. 140 pp.
Culture, Industrialisation and Education. G. H. Bantock. 108 pp.
*Education at Home and Abroad. Joseph Lauwerys and Graham Tayar. 144 pp.
Education, Work and Leisure. Harold Entwistle. 118 pp.
The Organization of Schooling: A Study of Educational Grouping Practices. Alfred Yates. 116 pp.
*Political Education in a Democracy. Harold Entwistle. 144 pp.
The Role of the Pupil. Barbara Calvert. 160 pp.
The Role of the Teacher. Eric Hoyle. 112 pp.
The Social Context of the School. S. John Eggleston. 128 pp.
The Sociology of Educational Ideas. Julia Evetts. 176 pp.

CURRICULUM STUDIES

*Towards a Compulsory Curriculum. J. P. White. 122 pp.

INTERDISCIPLINARY STUDIES

*Educational Theory: An Introduction. T. W. Moore. 116 pp.
Perspectives on Plowden. R. S. Peters. 116 pp.
*The Role of the Head. Edited by R. S. Peters. 136 pp.

* Library edition only

ING ALFRED'S COLLEGE
LIBRARY